THIS CERTIFICATE ENTITLES YOU TO

Two (2) Tickets to Self Made Live Hosted by Stefan Aarnio

Visit www.StefanAarnioLive.com for dates and locations.

These tickets are valued at $1295 each! Total value is $2590!

REGISTER NOW!
www.StefanAarnioLive.com

SELF MADE

CONFESSIONS OF A TWENTY-SOMETHING SELF MADE MILLIONAIRE

5 Secrets That Transform Ordinary People into Self Made Millionaires

Clovercroft Publishing

Self Made: Confessions of a Twenty-Something Self Made Millionaire

©2015 by Stefan Aarnio

Published by Clovercroft Publishing, Franklin, Tennessee.

Cover Design by Marla Beth Thompson

Cover photo by Lisa Waldner

Interior Design by Suzanne Lawing

Edited by Tammy Kling

Printed in Canada

978-1-942557-24-1

DEDICATION

This book is dedicated to anyone who looks up at the stars at night and wants more out of life. Your dream is out there, have the courage to seize it, and make your dream a reality.

No man is truly Self Made, but rather a synthesis of experiences and lessons from many others. It truly takes a village to raise a child. However, what remains undeniably Self Made is the human spirit. No team, no committee, no group of people can ignite the spark of desire in your heart or the glimmer in your eye that will make you take the first step toward greatness.

You are Self Made and you are on a journey. I salute you in the pursuit of your highest and greatest self.

Respect The Grind,

STEFAN AARNIO

"There is no chance, no destiny, no fate, that can circumvent or hinder or control the firm resolve of a determined soul."

ELLA WHEELER WILCOX

CONTENTS

FOREWORD

By: Frank McKinney

There is nothing nobler than the human desire to succeed, both for self and to share that success with others who are less fortunate. With a one-way plane ticket and $50 in my pocket, I left my small town in Indiana for Florida straight out of high school at age eighteen. I had a GPA of 1.8 (no hope of pursuing higher education), yet I had a million-dollar ambition. In my first job I dug sand traps on a Florida golf course—yes, a ditch digger!

So what does it take to make that million dollars of ambition a reality? It certainly takes guts, determination, an exercised risk threshold (your tolerance for risk), and most importantly, a Self Made spirit that sees any setback or failure as a challenge to change the mind of fate itself.

Twenty-five years ago I flipped my first crack house fixer-upper for $50,000 that I had purchased with money I had saved from my next job as a tennis instructor. Fast-forward 25 years (and many small houses in between) and I have successfully built or flipped over 30 oceanfront properties averaging $14,000,000 in sales price, with the crown jewel being an 18-bedroom, 24-bathroom, 16-car garage, 32,000-square-foot home for $50,000,000.

Others (Oprah, *20/20*, FOX, NBC, ABC, CBS, *USA Today* among many) say my journey has been meteoric and spectacular, from starting out as a tennis teacher with $50 in his pocket to transforming into a multimillionaire real-estate artist and maverick who builds and sells the most beautiful oceanfront "spec" homes in the world. If you didn't know, a spec home is a home built without a buyer. All risk, all day!

I've shared a little about myself, but this is all about my good friend Stefan Aarnio and the book that you are reading. Stefan reminds me very much of me and my early beginnings, yet he was light years ahead of me when I was his age!

I met Stefan in 2014 in Indianapolis at an all-day seminar I was hosting for my charity, The Caring House Project Foundation (www.chpf.org). Stefan generously donated a significant sum to CHP to attend my event, flying all the way from Winnipeg, Canada. To be honest, Stefan stood out like a sore thumb by sitting in the front row of the event and by wearing a full suit like a GQ model. Yet, I could tell he was serious about learning all he could by taking pages and pages of notes. His image may be quite different from mine, but my journey of personal transformation is strikingly similar to Stefan's as his story unfolds in the pages of this book.

I was a tennis instructor who saved up his earnings to get into real estate; Stefan was a guitar teacher who saved his earnings to get into real estate. I now live the life of a real-estate rock star; Stefan wanted to be a rock star when he was in his teens. I've been called a real-estate artist; Stefan is an artist who creates through his work. I started to make my fortune by flipping many small homes (most worth less than $100,000) and eventually multimillion dollar projects; Stefan has also made his fortune by flipping many small homes and, I have no doubt, will move up the price point ladder.

Making it big in life is not about where you start, but where you end up, and what you do for others. Our stories started the same and I have built a life of unimaginable success over the last 25 years by sticking to fundamental principles of success, many of which are outlined in Stefan's book. Although Stefan is young, he has achieved more success than most will in a lifetime. If you have a burning desire to make it big and become Self Made, then this book is for you.

I wish you all the best on your journey to success. There is much wisdom in the pages of this book: you are in good hands!

FRANK MCKINNEY
www.frank-mckinney.com
Real Estate Artist and
5x Best Selling Author

Part 1

A STRUGGLE OF THE SPIRIT

"Where there is no struggle, there is no strength."

OPRAH WINFREY

Confession #1

FOLLOW YOUR DREAMS
~~(CANCELLED)~~

*"Being a rock star is the intersection of who you are
and who you want to be."*

SLASH, GUNS N' ROSES

"I want to be a rock star," I told my dad.

"You what?" he replied, stunned.

The look on his face was more of a look of disbelief.

I was fifteen, with visions of being a rock star, playing my music at a deafening volume under bright lights and driving scores of girls wild as they would toss their bras onstage in adoration. I had no money to my name, but I had a million dollars of ambition and a burning desire to be rich and famous. Becoming rich seemed like the best option for my life—and the only way I knew that anyone could become rich was to become a rock star.

It was a youthful dream, centered on power and attention and wealth.

But it was my dream, so I set out on the path to achieve it and started playing in a band.

Musicians are some of the most vain, greedy, egotistical, and power-hungry people known to man. I was a musician who worked with musicians, surrounded myself with musicians, and lived with musicians… it was a chaotic lifestyle centered on freedom and nothing else. People who denounce the pursuit of power are often the most vicious power players, and although many musicians put up an artistic, peaceful, altruistic, loving, feel-good front, beneath it all is the lust for power and fame.

Rock stars can be seen as arrogant, and you can get a sense of their peacock character by looking at their dressing-room demands, such as soft carpet and eucalyptus bouquets (Rolling Stones), M&M's—no brown ones (Van Halen), and one of my favorites: Iggy Pop's request for the Seven Dwarfs to greet him at the entrance to his dressing room.

Early on, as I watched my parents work traditional jobs, I made up my mind. I was never going to have a real job. I was going to become a rich and famous rock star, travel the world, write my own songs, tell my own stories, and live an affluent, yet bohemian, life that others could only dream of. Of course, my parents wanted me to go to university and get a degree in economics or become a schoolteacher.

They wanted a profession that would guarantee me safety and security. But that didn't appeal to me at all!

And it doesn't appeal to me now.

Imagine the challenge for a young person today, with the lure of the entrepreneurial lifestyle, and reading stories of highly successful millennials in the tech sector and other industries. It must be difficult to focus on a traditional education compared with the myriad of inspiring and exciting options in the global economy.

It makes more sense to young people to pursue fame and fortune through music, acting, sports, or entrepreneurship than it does to "go to school and get a good job."

Children are smart.

If they spent their childhoods observing their parents working hard day in day out, slip deeper into debt after they went to school, and experienced higher education and "got good jobs," why would they want to do the same?

Many children see the struggle that their parents go through on a daily basis and grow up imagining there is a better way to earn a living and build a life.

After high school graduation, my parents divorced because my father wasn't earning enough money. He was a struggling entrepreneur who made a living, but not enough to make a life, so she left him. Of course, my mother will never say it was about the money, but she also said that if he had made more, things might have been different.

On a deeper level, the conflict between my parents evolved from the clash of ideology between my father's desire for an entrepreneurial lifestyle and my mother's desire for safety and security as a government teacher. Entrepreneurs are driven by freedom; government workers are driven by security. My mother got paid on the first and the fifteenth of the month, while some months, my father wouldn't bring home a paycheck. The instability irritated my mother, who was driven by security and she hated the fact that she worked hard and yet the family struggled to make ends meet.

Through this experience I learned that entrepreneurship is not for the faint of heart. It takes brains and guts to be successful.

Out of the wreckage left behind by my parent's separation, I chose to live with my mother because she was the more stable survivor. She said, "As long as you are going to university, you can live at home for free."

I quickly calculated the cost of rent and decided it was cheaper to pay university tuition each year and pursue my musical dreams than it was to rent an apartment or rent a room at home. Based strictly on the economics of free rent, I enrolled into the University of Manitoba's Jazz Studies program and began to live a double life.

At university I lived two lives: one was the life of a semi-keen music student and the other was that of an entrepreneur. Although I attended class and handed in all of my assignments and papers, I spent my discretionary time building my venture, my business, my key to freedom… my boat to sail the ocean of adventure—my rock band.

Like most entrepreneurs, my business consumed my consciousness every moment of every day. It was a love affair, an obsession, and at every opportunity available I would slip into fantasy to spend time with my one true love—rock 'n' roll.

School was my distraction and as the semesters went by, I dropped out of program after program. I initially enrolled in the Jazz Studies program but decided that living the life of a jazz musician was a gateway drug to living a dreadful life teaching high school band class, so I dropped out. Then I enrolled in the Asper School of Business, hoping to learn how to issue stock to the public because I wanted to get rich. I quickly found out that the school offered no such course and that attending the business school was the fast track to becoming a corporate middle manager. I envisioned myself bald and fat, aged forty-five, wearing a crisp white shirt while sitting at a large mahogany desk in a large corporation. The image killed my enthusiasm for the school of business.

In my first semester, I dropped out of my accounting class, got a D in Information Systems Management, and then decided that it was time to drop out of the business school all together.

Next I enrolled in Computer Science because I wanted to make video games. I spent half of my time in university working on my rock band and the other half playing video games. I played a lot of video games and figured, "Why not make them too?" I did really well in computer science, and even made a few primitive games, but I felt as though I was living in the wrong city to excel in the industry and I was still passionately in love with rock'n'roll, so, again, I dropped out. After dropping out of three faculties, I went into the office of the registrar at the university and asked:

"What do I have to do to get out of here without dropping out of school entirely?"

She smiled. "Take two English classes and you can finish with a degree in English!"

Standing there before her, as a student who had dropped out of three faculties, her words came as a relief. I didn't want to disappoint my parents completely by dropping out of school, even though my entire time at school had been an excuse to live at home rent-free, and I didn't want to be a failure, so instead of dropping out, I did the next best thing—I got an English degree.

Shortly after finishing two classes in poetry, I graduated from university with a Bachelor of Arts major in English with a minor in Music. Finally, I was free to pursue my secret love full-time without the distraction of school getting in the way.

Just when I thought I had a clear path to success, my mother reminded me that since I had graduated from school, it was time to "get a good job" and start paying her rent. I felt deflated with this news because my entire plan was to go to school, avoid paying rent, avoid getting a real job, and to somehow fulfill my fantasy of becoming a rock star all while skipping the realities of real life.

I reluctantly began to search for a job, and during my search I worked harder than ever on my rock band. Unfortunately for me the harder I pushed my band, the more resistance I got from my band mates. Trying to get four musicians to agree on an artistic and commercial direction for a group was like herding cats. As soon as I had lined up my "cats" in row, they would scatter and I would be chasing cats again.

I finally took a job selling luxury hotel rooms over the phone in the middle of the night on straight commission. The young lady running the human resources for the company was cheerful and pretty and promised me I would love working for the company. She also promised me that the company paid much higher wages and had more benefits than other competing companies. She wanted to make sure I had a degree, because the job was somewhat complex and they wanted smart and educated people working the phones. I assured her that I had all of her qualifications and she promptly offered me the job!

In the next few weeks I quickly learned that although I was a good salesman on the phone, the new commission structure that the company was experimenting on me paid me little more than minimum wage. I started work at 5 p.m. and finished work at 3 a.m. and keeping these graveyard hours isolated me from seeing any other human beings. Perhaps worse, when I got home from work, no one was available to talk to, no friends or family, in person or over the phone. Even the late night pizza places were closed. I felt like I was the last man on earth, living in a dark city where all of the other people had disappeared.

As I became isolated from the world, my rock band began to slowly drift apart, and my "safe, secure job" began to clutter and cloud my dreams of freedom. My spirit was dying and I began to lose my vision and vigor that I had when I was still a teenager.

Then, one day I got a call from one of my band mates.

"I'm leaving town," he said flatly.

"What?!" I hissed angrily.

"I'm going to plant trees. I need to make some money, and this band isn't really going anywhere." He paused and the roar of silence filled me ears. I wanted to scream. For months I had been herding cats, trying to put my music venture together, build a brand, build a sound, and build a following.

We were just starting to become successful, we had a potential band manager who wanted to work with us, and we had started getting some industry attention.

The pause dragged on and I was mute, with no rebuttal.

I realized that my band was dead—I couldn't operate without this key player.

My stomach sank, and I literally felt sick at the thought of my ruined hopes and dreams.

I had spent years of my life working on making the band a reality. To me it was a worthy and legitimate career. Time, money, blood, sweat, and tears had been poured into this labor of love and I could see that my band was becoming a Chinese finger trap—the harder I struggled, the harder it would squeeze me. I felt like I was drowning in quicksand and any sudden moves I made would drag me deeper and deeper until sand would fill my lungs and I would choke for my last breath of air.

OK. We're done," I muttered into the receiver and I hung up the phone.

I imagined he was surprised with my answer; I imagined he would expect me to struggle or argue with him or sell him on why we needed to keep going. But the truth was, I was exhausted, low on time, money, energy, effort—we both knew our venture wasn't working.

I hung up the phone, deflated.

SELF MADE LESSONS

1. Freedom vs. Security—what drives you? There is an inverse relationship between Freedom and Security. The more you gain of one, the more you lose of the other.

2. Business school creates employees, not entrepreneurs.

3. If you spend your time on Plan B (the English degree), you will never achieve Plan A (rock band)

4. No job can ever pay you what you are worth.

5. Follow Your Dreams ~~(Cancelled)~~: sometimes giving up on something that isn't working is the best thing that can ever happen to you.

Visit <u>SelfMadeConfessions.com</u> for more lessons.

Confession #2

YOUR BRAND-NEW EDUCATION IS OBSOLETE

"In this business it takes time to be really good—
and by that time, you're obsolete."

CHER

What happens when you experience the death of a dream?

Today I'd say move on, bounce back, and dream a new dream. Flowing water is formless and one of the most powerful forces on the planet; when it is blocked and cannot flow, it will seek a new direction or a new form. Formlessness is the strategy of many successful entrepreneurs. But at the same time, I was not formless like water; instead, I was brittle and resistant to change. In effect, change crushed me. The band had been my first real big dream, and it sank like the *Titanic* along with my spirit.

In the days that followed I was too tired to care and too tired to cry. I felt empty and tasted bitter defeat.

After hanging up the phone, I pivoted and allowed my exhausted body to fall onto my mother's couch like a felled tree and I just lay there for hours staring at the ceiling.

I lay on that couch for days and I didn't move, didn't shower, and didn't sleep. Some people would call it depression; I called it burnout. I just lay on the couch and watched the shadows and light move across the ceiling as time passed. I was so discouraged that life had reached a point of meaninglessness, and nothing made sense anymore.

I felt like an obsolete computer that had been tossed in the trash bin. I had been a loyal and compliant machine; I had faithfully gone down the assembly line of the entire education system from kindergarten through high school graduation and on to a post-secondary degree. I had gone to school; I had gotten a degree and I had a "good" job just like I was told. Just like a newly assembled computer, the moment I came off the assembly line, I was already obsolete. My immediate employment required a degree and I was earning minimum wage. The sad thing is that throughout school I had painted houses for summer work and earned more money than minimum wage.

I was more educated and more useless than ever before and worse—my one ray of hope for freedom, adventure, and economic salvation was extinguished.

I don't carry many conscious fears in my life, but one fear that overwhelmed me from deep within my soul was the feeling of becoming average.

Average.

Average is not excellent. Average is not what my mother had told me I would grow up to become. Average was not where I wanted to be.

In that moment on my mother's couch watching the shadows glide across the ceiling, I realized that I was no longer the guy with the cool band, or the cool concert promoter, or even a cool musician; I was now... just an average guy.

Fear is contagious; the more you fear something, the more likely you are to attract that which you fear. As I lay on my mother's couch, I had reached a point of maximum fear and I had manifested what I feared the most—I had become average. I had pursued "Plan B" so aggressively that "Plan A" died at birth. "Plan A" got swept aside and thrown in the trash bin as I poisoned my brilliant plans with average advice. I had taken a steady prescription of average advice from my teachers, parents, and peers for the first 20 years of my life and I was beginning to show side effects of stillborn average results. I vowed that I would stop taking average advice from average people and begin to take extraordinary advice from extraordinary people. Surely, this change would allow me to achieve extraordinary results.

I stayed there on my mother's couch for days like a wounded animal waiting to die. I was like a domesticated beast that had its teeth and claws painfully removed. I had no hunting instincts and could not survive in the jungle with my current skills. Like Pavlov's dog, which would salivate at the sound of a ringing bell, I had been trained by the school system to seek more education when faced with the problems of surviving in the real world.

As a lifetime student, all I knew how to properly do was read, research, write papers, and take tests. I didn't have the skills to survive in the wild, so I enrolled back into the sanctuary of university for a second degree. Disillusioned with education, I began to look for answers to my problem. My spirit was nearly dead and I realized that formal education could not provide answers to my problems, so I began to look for opportunities wherever I could find them.

One day in the underground university tunnel, I was scanning the gargantuan corkboards that seemed to run forever down the length of the subterranean tunnel. In the past when I scanned the corkboards, it was to find a spot to staple my rock'n'roll posters all over them. The board was littered with pieces of paper of all shapes, sizes, and colors into a beautiful mosaic of opportunities. Some pieces of paper were advertising rooms for rent; others had odd jobs or odd furniture for sale. One piece of paper in the sea of colors caught my eye. It read "Learn to be rich, just like Rich Dad Poor Dad." The poster had a picture of a purple and yellow book that sported the title "Rich Dad Poor Dad" in bold gold writing on a deep purple background.

I had passed this poster many times and had thought nothing of it. However, this time, I had the urge to read this book as I felt the emotions of my teenage ambition of fortune and fame flood my body. I immediately turned in the direction of the campus bookstore and located the mysterious book that spoke to my visceral desire to be rich.

I took it home, repositioned myself on my mother's couch, and began to read.

As my eyes scanned the pages of the book, I felt as though I had redis-covered rock'n'roll. It was the same way I had felt when I heard Jimi Hendrix play "Purple Haze" for the first time. I was like a deaf man who just regained his hearing and heard Led Zepplin after a life of deafness, or a blind man who just discovered the colors of Van Gogh. The book changed my entire paradigm of reality and I voraciously devoured it in one sitting.

New information and new truths became the building blocks of my new reality:

> Anyone can become rich.
> Getting rich is a science.
> Getting rich has little to do with luck.

Average Joes, like me lying on my mother's couch every day, can become fabulously wealthy through harnessing a few simple techniques and one of the most powerful asset classes known to man—real estate.

I didn't know how, I didn't know why, but in this moment, real estate became my new rock'n'roll.

Real estate became my passion, my obsession, my mistress that would visit me in the middle of the night. I went back to the bookstore and spent all of my available cash on books about real estate and making money in real estate. I would then take the piles of books back to my lair on mother's couch and mercilessly devour them one after the other. I would do this for days, weeks, and months, when I would do nothing but read, read, read, and read.

A new dream was born.

SELF MADE LESSONS

1. Average is dangerous, extraordinary is where the fortune lies.

2. Following average advice of average people will eventually lead you to average results.

3. In five years you will be the same person except for the books you read

and the people you meet.

4. The world is changing so fast today that our traditional education is often obsolete the moment we graduate. What are you doing to stay relevant in today's market economy?

Visit <u>SelfMadeConfessions.com</u> for more lessons.

Confession #3

MY FATHER SAID I WOULD NEVER BUY A PROPERTY

"Never give up, for that is just the place
and time that the tide will turn."

HARRIET BEECHER STOWE

Real estate became my muse… my lover, my focus, my business, my dream, my fuel, my gift, my reason to be.

I had a deep fascination and curiosity with this mysterious animal called real estate and I had to know how it worked. I had a deep desire to tame real estate like a wild beast and eventually become the master of it.

If the collapse of my rock band had been the fall of Rome, and my depression on the couch had been the Dark Ages, discovering real estate as a way to riches was my renaissance.

Rome was once a thriving and sophisticated society with literature, art, medicine, roads, and a sophisticated culture. After Rome fell to the barbarians, Europe collapsed into darkness and for at least 400 years, hardly a single European could read or write. The entire continent became illiterate.

For myself, my time on the couch was an illiterate time for dreams and an illiterate time for ambition. I still had a million dollars of ambition burning inside of me, but like an illiterate child, I had absolutely no way to express my desire. Discovering real estate was like becoming literate again, or at least discovering that I must become literate again.

When I decided at age sixteen to become a rock star, I learned the language of musical notes. I learned scales, arpeggios, modes, chords, triads, and how the fabric of music worked. Now that real estate had become my new rock'n'roll, I was illiterate once more. The words of real estate made no sense to me. Just like the tone deaf sixteen-year-old who could not make sense of melodies and sounds, I had to learn the new language of real estate.

As I embarked upon this new dream, I was astounded to learn just how illiterate I was with money, debt, finance, real estate, cash flow, and other terms. I learned that I did not understand this new language and neither did the rest of my family and friends.

I suddenly became a financial preacher, preaching financial literacy to anyone and everyone who would or would not listen. I started to lose friends and began to alienate the people in my life with my new language and wisdom. I became even more isolated because I didn't practice what I preached and to many, I appeared to be crazy.

One night I was at my father's house for dinner and I managed to recite every single fact that I had learned about making money in real estate. My father looked at me with a tired, blank look on his face and said,

"Real estate is a fad. You know music, stick to music. This is just your flavor of the week. You will never buy a property!"

His words stung.

Although I was in my twenties, I felt a teenage rebellion rise up within me.

My father had been very supportive of my musical endeavors and my formal education at university. Why was he suddenly so offensive toward my newfound passion of real estate and the science of getting rich?

In the moment, I didn't understand why my father was so negative toward my real-estate ambitions and later learned that he had wanted to make his wealth in real estate but had three major barriers to entry. My father had wanted to make money in real estate with zero cash, zero credit, and zero experience. My mother was unsupportive of his real-estate ambitions and she killed his dream before it got off the ground. I began to face the harsh reality of my situation—to make money in real estate, I needed to secure cash, credit, and experience to make my dreams a reality.

It occurred to me that I had the same three problems my father had.

I had absolutely no real experience with property and all of my dealings with real estate had been fantasies up to this point. My lack of tangible experience in the real-estate industry triggered an insatiable hunger for knowledge that began to spiral out of control. Instead of taking action and jumping into the market feet first, I began to poison myself with "analysis paralysis." I was alone on my journey to buy real estate; none of my musician friends showed any interest in making money in real estate. My family was clearly uninterested and I was alone consuming real-estate books like an alcoholic consumes his drink, alone and in the dark. If only I had a partner to take the first steps with me, I would be able to move forward, but fear of the unknown paralyzed me and my only solution seemed to be to consume more information.

They say that the definition of insanity is to "do the same thing over and over again and expect a different result." At this point in my life, I was the poster boy for insanity. I had read in one of my real-estate books that taking a seminar or a class on real-estate investing was one of the best ways to break into the market. The book warned me in advance that these classes were expensive, but I decided to make a move and in my moment of decision, and I began to feel my disease of analysis paralysis begin to lift. I was determined to save up nearly all of my spare cash and take a real-estate seminar to learn the missing pieces of the puzzle and alleviate my fears. I immediately put into action an aggressive saving plan and began saving 70% of my income. Every single expense was slashed and I was living on barely the basics. Riding the bus to school on a student pass became a necessity and making phone calls from my mother's landline was embarrassing.

I eventually saved a few thousand dollars and one fateful afternoon after my classes at school, I saw an online ad advertising that Donald Trump, the real-estate billionaire, was going to be teaching a seminar in my local area. I immediately signed up for the free class and felt as though I was moving ahead with my dream of getting rich in real estate.

The days flew by and when the day of the free seminar came, I borrowed my mother's red station wagon and drove it to the airport hotel that was hosting the free event. I parked the car and was quickly herded into a hotel banquet room like a cow in a cattle line. I found a seat near the front and eagerly awaited the presentation. One of my adult guitar students, and a business school classmate, was also attending, so he took a seat next to me. There we sat at the front of the room, ready to see Donald Trump and learn real estate from the master himself.

As the room filled up, a speaker took the stage. This man was slick, well groomed with a moustache, a dark tan, and a perfectly pressed suit. He took the stage with the vigor and confidence of a circus ringmaster and informed us that Donald Trump would not be in attendance that night, but a video playing on the screen behind him had a prerecorded video of Donald himself endorsing the circus ringmaster. As ridiculous as it all seems in hindsight, at the time, the experience seemed legitimate to me.

The speaker then spent the next hour and a half showing us case study after case study where Donald Trump made millions of dollars for himself and where the speaker himself made tens of thousands of dollars flipping houses all over the United States. As his presentation came to a close, he offered the crowd Donald Trump's Real Estate University, where in 2 days, he would teach us all of Donald's secrets. The price of that weekend was $3,000 but that day, and that day only (the speaker reassured us), the weekend was only $1,500. My heart began to beat wildly as this seemed too good to be true and exactly what I was looking for. I was stuck; reading books had only got me so far in my quest to purchase investment real estate and I had saved enough cash to afford this one seminar.

People began getting out of their seats and running to the back of the room to take advantage of this "once in a lifetime opportunity." I got up calmly and my business school classmate looked at me in disbelief and said, "Are you actually going to do this?" He didn't believe that the words of the speaker were true and was clearly very skeptical of the entire operation. I, on the other hand, had come to the event with the intention of purchasing a real-estate education.

I was so nervous that I felt sick, but appeared to confidently and slowly walk to the back of the room to fill out an order form for the course. As I swiped $1,500 on my credit card, I felt my commitment level increase tenfold and I knew that there was no turning back now. The event staff handed me a large plastic bag filled with binders and other educational materials to study before I took the course in thirty days. I left the airport hotel with my adrenaline pumping. I had committed to make a real change in my life and this was one of the first major steps. It was now nearly 11:00 p.m. at night and I drove my mother's station wagon home on the empty streets under the city street lamps.

As I rolled into my mother's driveway, I parked the car in the garage, entered the pitch black, silent house, and slowly crept up the stairs to my room. As I was about to take my bag of precious materials to my bedroom and go to bed, I decided that out of pride, I would wake my mother up and tell her what I had done. My mother's room was across the hall from mine, and the door was open, yet the hallway and her room were pitch black.

I poked my head inside the door to my mother's room and whispered:

"Mom!"

"Mom!"

"Mom!"

"What!?" she whispered back; I could hear her and knew she was sleeping, but I saw nothing but darkness.

"I bought a real-estate course tonight!"

"You what?!" she replied, waking up faster than I could anticipate.

"I bought a real-estate course!" I replied.

"How much was it?!" she inquir, sounding skeptical and even fearful for my decision.

"Fifteen hundred dollars," I replied, trying to stay cool and not absorb her fear.

"FIFTEEN HUNDRED DOLLARS?! ARE YOU CRAZY!? THAT'S TOO MUCH!" She turned the lights on and sat up in bed, staring at me like I had summoned her deepest fears.

"That's how much it was." I started to backpedal. I felt as though I had made a mistake and started to sweat. She turned the lights on to glare at me and after feeling her cold gaze penetrate into my skull, I turned the lights off and disappointedly closed the door.

I went to my room, dropped my sack of course materials on the floor, and felt fear and panic take over. Had I done the right thing? Had I wasted all of my savings on this speculative course? Was she right? Or was she just trying to protect me from financial predators who sell overpriced courses?

I couldn't sleep that night; I was so confidant I had done the right thing, but she had shaken my confidence to the core. Although I was shaken, I was not broken, and the next day, I began to study the course materials that were provided and I galvanized my commitment to learning how to make my fortune in real estate.

The day of the course came sooner than I had anticipated and although I had invited many of my friends and family to join me as a guest for free, no one wanted to learn the secrets of real estate. After inviting everyone I knew and facing rejection after rejection, my younger brother tagged along and the two of us attended the class together. Although I knew a lot about music at this point in my life, I knew nearly nothing about real estate.

For the entire weekend, I focused as hard as I could and learned about mortgages, cash flow, down payments, cap rates, and other terms that apply to investing in real estate. The hours flew by, but I wasn't absorbing the information as fast as I wanted. It seemed that the more I learned at the class, the more I discovered that I didn't know. By the end of the weekend, I felt as though I had poured salt on a wound and rather than making myself feel more confident to purchase my first property, I felt more confused and even more paralyzed than before.

At the end of the weekend, the seminar promoters offered a mentorship package for $30,000 where they would work with me one-on-one to put a live real-estate deal together. My heart sank because I wanted a mentor to help me so badly but had absolutely no cash to my name and my credit card only had a $500 limit on it. My mother was right. I had wasted my money and I walked out to the parking lot empty handed and cried like a baby out of frustration. I knew where I was, I knew where I needed to go, and I couldn't find a way to get there. One thing was for certain: I did not have access to $30,000 and I was too ashamed of myself to ask anyone for help.

I was back to the drawing board; I had consumed an inordinate amount of books, had spent all of my money on a real-estate seminar, and still had come out empty handed. A normal person would quit at this point and go on with their life, but not me; I was obsessed. Real estate had become an obsession and it had captivated me the same way music had captivated me when I was 16 years old. Instead of quitting, I committed even harder to my cause and began to read even more and study between 5 and 8 hours a day.

My mother's couch, where I had lain depressed for months over the death of my rock star dream, became a fortress of books on investing, business, real estate, and personal development. If I wasn't at school, I was on the couch reading. If I wasn't teaching guitar, I was on the couch reading. If I wasn't sleeping, I was on the couch reading. My resolve was unwavering, my commitment was increasing, and more than anything else, I wanted to prove all of my doubters, including my family, to be wrong.

Along with increasing my commitment to devouring as many books as I could get my hands on, I also kept saving most of my earnings for more seminars. I knew that my inability to take action was only temporary, and I felt as though I had tried to tame a wild stallion and had been thrown off the horse. I committed to myself that no matter how many times I would be thrown off the horse, I would get back up and try again. As the Japanese proverb says, "Fall down seven times, get up eight."

To supplement my fortress of books, I began to attend any and every seminar on real estate, whether it was free or a paid event. I began to attend so many events that I would see the same group of seminar junkies roam from room to room. We were addicts, all searching for a solution to our common money problems and attended the seminars like support groups, hoping each and every time to have a new addiction breakthrough. Of course, many of these junkies were just junkies roaming the landscape of books, tapes, and seminars, hoping to find a way to get rich quick and solve their money problems. I saw the pattern of these people and vowed to observe them, but never to copy them; I needed to do something different.

SELF MADE LESSONS

1. Any new skill brings new words and a new language.

2. Giving unsolicited advice to people who do not want it is one of the easiest ways to "lose friends and alienate people."

3. People with dead dreams will try to kill yours; sometimes it's best to keep your dreams a secret (even from family).

4. Analysis paralysis is a disease where we forgo taking action in favor of collecting more information. Collect 70% of the information you need and then take action!

5. Save a portion of your cash each month for further education. School is never finished for the professional.

6. If you think education is expensive, try ignorance.

7. Your birth family will not always support your dreams; find people who are chasing the same dream and form a spiritual family.

Visit SelfMadeConfessions.com for more lessons.

Confession #4

HE WHO GIVES
THE MOST WINS

"As my dad said, you have an obligation to leave
the world better than how you found it. And he also
reminded us to be givers in this life, and not takers."

PHIL CRANE

My consumption of real-estate material and books had reached a saturation point; I started to realize that no matter how much I read, reading would never get me off the couch. I had attended a few seminars on real estate, but was still paralyzed by fear of buying an actual property. Although I was scared, I knew that if I kept my activity high, eventually, I would meet the right person or find the right opportunity. Some of the seminar junkies I had met began to form support groups to hold each other accountable. We wanted to support each other to take action on some of the techniques we had learned but had failed to put into practice. We would meet in basements around the city like resistance fighters fighting a common foe—our own fear, weaknesses, and ignorance. We met secretly to feel like we belonged to something special, perhaps an elite club, but in truth, we met secretly to connect with like-minded individuals and avoid the ridicule of our friends and families.

Sometimes the people who are closest to you can hurt you the most.

Everyone wants to see their friends get ahead, but they don't want to see their friends get ahead of them! Our friends and families were like a bucket of crabs. The second one of the crabs would have a breakthrough and appear to be climbing out of the bucket, the other crabs, namely our friends and family, would reach up with their claws and pull us back down into the bucket. I felt the crab bucket effect with my own friends and family. Instead of helping me get ahead, helping me learn, grow, or change, my closest friends would drag me down into the bucket of sameness.

At one of these support groups, late one Wednesday night, I met another junkie named Tony. Tony was in his early thirties, married, and had pale skin, red hair, and freckles. He was a very genuine guy, cared about the well-being of other people and had just quit his job as an engineer to sell real-estate investments for a seminar company. Tony was a believer; he believed in financial education and that the school system had failed to educate the ignorant population on money and investing. Tony wanted to bring justice to the world by educating his clients on real estate, money, and investing. I could see that Tony believed that quitting his job was the right thing to do. He believed his pursuit was noble and hid his fear well behind a thin veil of confidence.

Tony and I gravitated toward each other naturally, like magnets. He was one of the youngest guys in the room in his early thirties and I was by far the baby in the room in my early twenties. Very quickly, almost too quickly, Tony invited me to come with him and his wife to attend a real-estate seminar in Edmonton the following weekend. He offered me a ticket for $100. The admission was normally $500, but since he had just started working for the event promoter, I could come for a fraction of the sticker price. I had very little money, but decided that I was committed to my path of learning everything I could about money and real estate, so the following weekend I showed up at Tony's house at 5 a.m. It was pitch black except for the dim glow of the street lamps, and the October air was getting colder. Tony and his wife crammed into his tiny Honda Civic with suitcases, food, and supplies. Somehow I folded my tall, thin body in the backseat and sat sideways so my legs could fit. We started to drive west on the 16-hour journey to Edmonton with only brief stops to buy energy drinks and use the bathroom.

I hardly knew anything about Tony and his wife, Mandy, but I trusted them because we believed the same things. In truth, Tony could have been a serial killer, but our shared beliefs were so strong that I didn't bother checking into his background. Tony and I believed that we had been left ignorant about money by the education system and we believed that we needed financial education to become financially free one day. We both shared the mutual dream of not having to work for money and to wake up in the morning and have money appear magically in the mailbox without working. We knew that we were not going to reach our dreams at our current jobs and felt so strongly about our beliefs that we were willing to wake up in the middle of the night, cram into close quarters, and drive across the country together to chase a common dream.

With Tony being an analytical engineer, and very detail oriented, he had prepared for the weekend much better than I had. Tony was an information junkie like me and had prepared a stack of audiobooks that we would listen to in the car along with snacks and plenty of topics to talk about. I, on the other hand, had left the house with only $100 cash in my pocket, didn't make a budget for the weekend, and had acted on emotion more than logic. I brought almost nothing with me and between my ragged jeans and long hair, if you took a quick glance at me, I might have been mistaken for a homeless wanderer. One of the first books we listened to as we drove across the country was *The 4 Hour Work Week* by Tim Ferris. The book expanded my mind to a new size as I absorbed life-changing advice about becoming rich in the new economy. One piece of advice that stuck with me immediately was: "If you aren't successful, try the opposite and you will likely be a success." I decided that my life so far had been a failure; my band had failed, I had an unwanted and overpriced university degree, I wasn't making enough money to live, and I had a very basic lifestyle. As I took inventory of my life so far, I knew that my current situation was a mess and if I didn't change, I would be stuck forever. I decided to take the author's advice to heart and made the decision that this weekend, I would do the opposite of what I normally would do and see if there was truth to the "opposite" theory. During the 16-hour car ride, I reflected on my life so far and realized that I had been a "taker" and not a "giver" and that I would make it my mission this weekend to give more than I was to receive.

As Tony's Honda Civic rolled into the parking lot of the hotel in Edmonton, we began to make dinner plans. I only had $100 cash on me for the entire trip and I had to buy nearly 16 meals for myself with that budget. I did the math in my head and knew that my $100 was not going to last three full days of breakfasts, lunches, and dinners at restaurants, especially if I had to buy drinks and tip the waitresses. With my poverty mentality, I hated tipping at restaurants, but had been socially pressured into paying extra T.I.P.S "To Insure Prompt Service." I wanted to leave my poverty mentality behind forever, so I decided to try the opposite of what I would normally do.

The very first night as we were settling into our hotel, I offered to buy Tony and Mandy dinner. The hotel we were staying at had pizza flyers in the room, so I ordered a lavish meal that was way out of my budget for the evening. I focused on being as generous as possible and spared no expense: pizza, wings, salads, and drinks promptly arrived to the room. I felt grateful and wanted to add value to my hosts for looking after me. The dinner cost me $40 and nearly 40% of my food budget before the weekend had even started, but I felt as though it was the right thing to do and it was certainly the opposite of what I would normally do.

My poverty mentality wanted me to go to McDonalds for every meal and eat the cheapest cheeseburgers off the cheapest menu to stretch my dollars for the whole weekend to make my budget last for the whole weekend or maybe more. Since I had made the decision to "do the opposite," this poverty plan was no longer an option. Instead of being cheap, I decided to be generous and give away more than I could afford.

Somehow, my generosity paid off and the next morning when we were attending the seminar, Tony informed me that my $100 admission was waived and that I could now attend for free. I also learned that the entire weekend was catered for breakfast and lunch and suddenly, I felt the wisdom of the lesson sink in. I had taken care of Tony and Mandy by buying dinner the night before, and now they were taking care of me. My poverty desire to be cheap and save money was beginning to melt away and I began to see the world in terms of value and instead of cost.

The lenses through which I saw the world were beginning to change and my old viewpoint would never return. The wealth principle of "giving" instead of "taking" was settling in and I decided to push my theory to the limit and force myself to act in the opposite direction of my poverty mind for the rest of the weekend.

Over a dozen speakers spoke at the weekend, each preaching their own formula for great riches. After every speaker spoke, I approached them, thanked them, and told them about what I loved about their presentation. Each and every speaker was grateful to hear some praise and would give me a free copy of their book. These free books were completely unexpected, but because I gave the speakers praise, they reciprocated with a book. By the end of the weekend, I had a stack of nearly a dozen free books that I received just from giving thanks. I was so appreciative of the event that I thanked the promoter, praised him for taking care of all of the fine details of an event, and genuinely told him that the event was the best I had ever attended. The promoter immediately reciprocated and invited me personally to his house for dinner later that evening. As the evening advanced, I noticed that I was the only non-staff member present for dinner.

By the end of the weekend, I had made friendships for life, planted the seeds for relationships that would turn into business partnerships, collected over a dozen books, and still had $40 left of my original $100 food budget. The wealth principle of giving more than receiving became real to me and I was astounded by the extra value I had created with only appreciation, praise, and gratitude. I had changed my thinking from a "taker" to a "giver" and had done such a good job of "giving" that I had created a real money surplus for myself.

With my last $40, I gave the cash to Tony and Mandy for gas. It was literally all I had and I was more than happy to add any final value to them that I could. The $100 I spent that weekend was one of the best $100 I ever spent. I learned a lesson that I could never forget—to be wealthy, we must give, not take. Wealth is generated when we create value and share. I still cringe today at the thought of hoarding my $100 and sitting alone in McDonalds eating cheap cheeseburgers. Had I done that, my life would be drastically different today. Little did I know that my decision to leave the poverty mind behind that weekend would make me millions of dollars over the rest of my life.

SELF MADE LESSONS

1. Going to seminars and reading books is no substitute for taking action.

2. One of the best ways to build your network and meet like-minded

people is through seminars.

3. When something doesn't work, try the opposite. Trying the opposite is one of the quickest ways to turn failure into success.

4. He who gives the most usually gets the most.

5. By giving intangible value like thanks and gratitude, you can stretch $100 of cash into hundreds of dollars of value. Value doesn't always have to be tangible.

6. Practicing gratitude is one of the fastest ways to stop a poverty mentality and transform into a wealth mentality.

Visit <u>SelfMadeConfessions.com</u> for more lessons.

Confession #5

MY PARENTS GAVE ME TWO GREAT GIFTS

"When I was growing up, my parents told me,
'Finish your dinner. People in China and India are starving.'
I tell my daughters, 'Finish your homework. People in India
and China are starving for your job.'"

THOMAS FRIEDMAN

My parents gave me two great gifts: my mother gave me a high self-esteem and my father gave me a map of "what not to do" with my life.

My dad read car magazines, and he didn't make any investments in learning or personal development. My father never made the investments into himself that were required to succeed in the ultracompetitive game of business. To be successful entrepreneurs, personal development is like oxygen. He never bothered to hire a coach, go to a seminar, or read a book. He just tried to do things his own way.

Although my father became my example of "what not to do," I made many of the same life choices that he did.

That's often a part of life... right?

You learn from other people's mistakes. And then, you must learn from your own.

Through watching my father struggle, he gave me a map of how he did the "right things" in the "wrong way."

My father was an entrepreneur who craved the freedom and income that entrepreneurship could afford. Every day, people quit their jobs with the seductive idea in their mind that they will "be their own boss" or "work from home." These people want to reach "unlimited earning potential." However, 90% of these people fail within five years of entering the jungle of the real world. Of the survivors, 90% of the remaining entrepreneurs fail in the second five years. In many ways, entrepreneurship is the highest risk and highest reward game available for anyone to play.

My father saw the upside of entrepreneurship and had a dream of reaping the bountiful fruits of his labor while being the captain of his own ship. He grew up with an entrepreneurial father who ran a foundry in Finland and understood what an entrepreneur's life should look like. As a young boy, my father would go to the foundry with his father and watch the employees work, see the equipment, watch his father pay the payroll, and see the sparkle in his father's eyes when his company would produce a beautiful product. Somehow my father caught the entrepreneurial bug and brought it with him to Canada.

When I was a young boy, I grew up around boxes of T-shirts and sweatshirts that were piled up in the basement and the garage of our family home. My father ran a promotional products business out of our house and later expanded to lease a building in a derelict industrial part of town.

When my parents would send me to school, I often had 12-inch rulers that my father had misprinted. These rulers read "Govurnement" instead of "Government" because a customer had failed to proofread the sample. I also had sample highlighters from promotional sample books and sample pens as school supplies. My pencil case looked like a promotional products show room. In the summer when school was out, I would be hired to sweep the dirt off the steps of my father's building and clean decades of dust out of the old industrial shop that they had just moved into. My dad's business was a big part of my childhood, whether I realized it or not at the time.

I caught the entrepreneurial bug during these formative years with my father. As a seven-year-old, I loved to draw; I would draw space aliens, space ships, and medieval battles. I had stacks of artist coil bound books filled with my drawings piled up in my room and I would show my latest drawings to my parents when the ink was dry.

One Saturday morning I showed my parents a picture of two space aliens that I had drawn. My mother, always so supportive of any of my creations (no matter how horrible), praised my artistic talent and attention for detail. My father also offered me praise and then asked if I would like to put my design on a T-shirt.

I had grown up literally surrounded with boxes of printed shirts all over the house and loved the idea of printing my design onto a run of T-shirts.

"Let's do it!" I looked up at my father, with excitement in my eyes.

"OK," said my father. "We will print a run of shirts and you can sell them to your friends at school."

The venture sounded very exciting to me, so I gave my father the drawing of the aliens and he took it to work to have the T-shirts made up.

My first venture, with a product I had produced, was underway and within eight weeks, a huge white cardboard box filled with white T-shirts arrived in my house.

I tore the box open and pulled out a soft white cotton T-shirt. I held the shirt up and stretched it out and felt the black ink of my design that had literally been baked into the fabric of the shirt.

I took a sample shirt to my third grade class for show-and-tell and held it up for the 30 kids in the room to see. As a natural salesman, I praised the quality of the cotton, and I told the room that the shirt was locally sourced and quality made. I even let the other kids touch the ink that was burned onto the shirt. To top it all off, I told a story I had made up about my design and the alien creatures I had put on the shirt.

The class was sold.

The orders poured in and very quickly; my box of T-shirts that my father had advanced on "dad credit" were sold out. The shirts cost less than $5 to print and I sold them for $20. At the age of eight, my mind and my perceptions of money were changing forever. Without knowing what I was doing, I had learned to design a product, make a run of product on credit, and sell in front of a room of prospective buyers. My first "no money down" deal was a success. I had been successful at my first business venture and I knew I could never turn back.

My awareness of the importance of saving money came at a young age as well. Throughout my childhood and early teens, I developed a cash mentality. My grandmother would quiz me every birthday when she would hand me an envelope with a $20 bill in it. She would ask, "And what are you going to do with the money?" I had been trained by my mother, father, and grandmother to say, "I'm going to put it in the bank!" and so I did.

My father tried to explain why we put our money in the bank, but always left me confused. "If you put a dollar in the bank, it earns interest, and that interest compounds and eventually you will have your money making money."

"What's interest, Dad?" I asked.

"It's when the bank pays you a rental fee to leave your money with them so that they can lend it out to other people. The bank buys and sells money, and in your case, you are renting your money to them."

"How much interest will they pay me?" I inquired, suddenly interested in the concept of my money earning extra money.

"One or 2 percent," my father said. "That's how people get rich, investing their money."

I thought about what my father had told me. One or 2 percent meant that if I left my $100 of birthday money in the bank, in a year, I would have $101. That idea did not appeal to me very much at all; even as a young child I felt that a 1% gain did not make sense. Rich people, or people with a lot of money, must be earning more than 1% per year!

My child logic, my common sense refused to accept my father's words as truth.

I thought about the bank even more. If I won the lottery and made $1,000,000, at 1 or 2 percent, I would only be earning $10,000 to $20,000 per year and that seemed more interesting to my child appetite for money, but where and how was I going to get my hands on $1,000,000 to leave with the bank? I had many small ventures that earned me many small amounts of money, but I knew that I would never be able to save my way to $1,000,000. People who were rich certainly weren't just saving their way to millions? Were they?

Like a good son and with my father's words in my head, I kept up the saving mentality for years. Whenever I earned money from my T-shirt businesses, babysitting, running a small lemonade stand, or later guitar teaching business, I would put the money in the bank or hide the cash in my room if I didn't want to pay banking fees, which I felt were robbery. I understood, like most entrepreneurs, that I did not know when my next payday was coming, so I had to bank up and store the cash. If I wanted to buy a guitar or a skateboard, I would have to earn the money somehow and pay cash. There was no credit for me and my cash mentality grew with me into my adult years. There was no such thing as credit, unless it was to do a run of T-shirts, so I always had to save up and divide my dollars to make sure I would not run out of money.

Living outside my means was not an option.

My father was a frugal immigrant and I inherited the frugal, maybe even cheap, immigrant mentality.

Every month when the bank would send me a statement of my account, I reviewed it very carefully to make sure that there were no errors and that my income always dramatically exceeded my expenses. I also made sure I kept enough cash in my account to avoid banking fees, which even as a twelve-year-old boy, I felt were an unjust way for the bank to steal my money.

As I grew up, I avoided buying a car, because I could not afford to buy one with cash. I wanted to avoid a monthly car payment as well, so riding the bus each day was my best option. I avoided buying a cell phone until I became a full-time real-estate investor because of my strong cash mentality and desire to keep expenses low.

With my immigrant cash mentality, I was able to scrimp and save up to 70% of my income and I avoided all types of credit like the plague. To me, cash was freedom, and as long as I avoided monthly costs like cars and cell phones, I would have the freedom to earn as much or as little as I wanted and survive for an indefinite amount of time should I fail to earn any money.

My cash-only mentality served me well for years until I began to develop a definite desire to be rich.

I had scrimped and saved my way through university. I rode the bus, I wore second-hand clothing from thrift stores, I kept my expenses as close to zero as possible, and anything I did buy was justified as a tax write-off for my guitar-teaching business or my rock band business. I had been frugal for years and had built a small nest egg of cash in my bank account, but I had reached the point where frugal began to turn into cheap.

Frugal people are able to purchase value or have real value for less. For example, buying a $400 pair of quality Italian leather shoes for $100 is frugal; buying a $10 pair of fake leather knock-offs at Wal-Mart is cheap. The $400 shoes will last a lifetime if they are looked after, look amazing, and build social status, while the $10 Wal-Mart shoes will fall apart after three months and everyone will know that you are cheap and cannot understand value.

My frugality began to turn into cheapness when I began to desire real estate. Properties at the time in my city were $50,000, $100,000, or $200,000 and I knew that I had to buy real estate if I wanted to be rich. Unfortunately, with my cash-flow situation, I did not have enough cash to make a purchase! All wealth in the world is either made or held in real estate and I believed this wisdom with every molecule of my being. This desire vibrated through my body and into my soul.

I wanted to be wealthy and live a life of freedom more than ever before.

I rode the bus to and from university every day and I would sit on the dirty, smelly, bus bench and read sheet after sheet of property listings in the real-estate news. I would scan the thumbnails of properties for properties that I believed would make me a monthly income to replace my guitar teacher earnings.

"$50,000 duplex, rents for $1,200 per month," the ad would say. I would read the numbers stated in the ads and would scribble down some math on a scrap piece of paper I kept next to me on the bus. I would calculate that a property like this would put a few hundred dollars of extra income in my pocket every month and would supplement my low musician income.

This property would be the first stepping-stone toward my financial freedom and my pursuit of being rich. As the bus rolled down the road from the university toward my mother's house, I decided to pull the string signaling the driver to let me off at the bank. I stepped off the bus and folded the real-estate news under my arm like a rolled up newspaper and began to walk up the front steps of my local bank.

"What was I going to say?" I thought; I didn't have $50,000 to buy this property, but I desperately wanted to buy it. Since I didn't have enough cash, I decided that I would ask the bank for a mortgage.

My logic was good; I had a monthly income that was steady and predictable while I also had enough cash for an acceptable down payment. I had banked with my bank for years and the same amount of money was deposited into my checking account every single month at the same time. I knew I could afford to pay the mortgage for this property; even if it was vacant, and I even had extra money to carry the property if I had to. This was going to be my first investment property and I was finally on my way to becoming financially free!

I sat down with my banker and enthusiastically showed him the numbers I had scribbled down on a scrap piece of paper and unfolded the real-estate news to show him a picture of the property I wanted to buy. I explained that I had enough money for a down payment and that I had enough income to cover the mortgage even if the property was vacant and that I would be earning an extra $1,200 per month in rent.

At the end of my short, disorganized, yet enthusiastic pitch, my banker looked at me and said, "Let me check your credit." He typed my name into the computer and looked at my records. I sat in the chair across from him for what seemed like an eternity. As time passed, I began to slouch while he looked deeper and deeper into my credit history.

"Hmmmmm... I'm sorry, we can't lend to you." He looked at me with a thin, apologetic smile on his face.

"Why not?!" I exclaimed. "I have the money, I have the income. I can afford this property!"

"Well, that may be true," he continued, "but you don't have any established credit with the bureau, so we can't give you a mortgage."

"How do I build credit?!" I stammered, seeing my opportunity and dreams slowly slip out of reach.

The loan officer tapped on the keyboard. "Well, let me sign you up for a credit card. You're a student, right?"

"Yeah, I'm a student, but I don't want a credit card. I'm an all-cash kind of guy! I hate debt, I'm never going into debt. Debt is evil!"

"Look," said the banker, "do you want to build credit and get a mortgage to buy this property or not? Just because you have a credit card doesn't mean you have to carry a balance or pay interest. Just because you have credit doesn't mean you have to go into debt." The banker looked at me with a smile. "Just buy Coke and chips every month on this card, and then come into the bank and pay it off with cash. After 6 months, you will have a credit score and we can lend to you."

I was intrigued by his proposition, but hated the idea of buying anything on credit and then paying it off with cash. What if I mismanaged my money? What if I forgot? What if I spent too much? What if I lived outside my means? What if I couldn't pay? All of these thoughts raced through my head. My cash mentality was so strong, I resisted the idea of having a credit card, but ultimately, my desire to buy property won me over and I signed the freshly printed credit application.

I slid the signed papers to the banker across the desk and he typed in a few more bits of information to his computer.

"Congratulations! You are approved! Because we can't verify your income and because you are a student, we can only give you $500 at this time, but as you build up your credit, we'll give you more. You should receive your new card in the mail with your name on it later this week. That wasn't so bad, was it?" The banker smiled at me again and held out his hand to shake mine.

"Thanks," I said.

I shook his hand and smiled. But as I turned and walked out of the bank, my stomach was tied in a knot.

My cash-is-king mentality was dead.

It was the end of an era.

SELF MADE LESSONS

1. Ninety-nine percent% of entrepreneurs fail in the first 10 years of business—to survive you need a competitive advantage. If you don't have a competitive advantage in your business, get out of that business and find a new one.

2. A wise man learns from his mistakes while a genius learns from other people's mistakes.

3. As an entrepreneur, you never know when your next payday is. You must save your cash and build a large reserve.

4. Know the difference between frugal and cheap. Frugal is driven by value, cheap is driven by cost.

5. Building credit with credit cards is one of the fastest and easiest ways to build credit.

Visit SelfMadeConfessions.com for more lessons.

Confession #6

KNOWLEDGE IS THE TICKET OUT OF POVERTY

"Knowledge is power. Information is liberating. Education is the premise of progress, in every society, in every family."

KOFI ANNAN

An immigrant is four times more likely to become a millionaire than a native-born American. Some may wonder why immigrants are more likely to become millionaires, but we forget that selling everything you own and packing up to move to a foreign land is the most entrepreneurial thing that anyone can do!

When you have to start over, you learn the skills of a street fighter: tenacity, persistence, watching your back, seeing what others don't see. Entrepreneurs never give up. They know they are the ones responsible for putting money in the bank and food on the table. For a true hardcore entrepreneur, making money is a survival instinct.

The most reliable way for anyone to become a millionaire is investing and entrepreneurship.

As the son of an entrepreneur, I grew up around a real live business and worked both on the business and in the business. I carried boxes, and learned how to sweep floors, count inventory, and later design web sites for my father's business. For me, entrepreneurship wasn't a choice or something that students dissected on the operating table of a business school; entrepreneurship was raw, dirty, and a natural way of life.

As a child, I always had a deep curiosity for how things worked. At age seven, I taped two large cardboard boxes together and built a lever into the machine. When I pulled the lever, the machine would pour me a glass of Coca-Cola. I even cut a hole in the front of the machine for customers to put coins into so I could collect money and pour Coca-Cola or 7UP depending on what the customer wanted. I was fascinated with knowing how Coke machines and gumball machines worked and I also wanted to collect the nickels, dimes, and quarters inside.

As I grew, I either built small business ventures or did odd jobs for cash. I never kept a steady job with a boss, pay stub, and deductions. Instead, I had customers who I would do work for, earn cash, and then I would bank the cash I earned. Everything was cash, there was no debt, and I operated this way because I knew deep down in my heart that as long as I was personally debt-free, I was a free man.

I only began to operate with debt and credit when I began to have a desire to purchase real estate and earn a residual income. Only when I wanted to buy things I couldn't afford, like a $100,000 property, did I begin to use credit and debt to my advantage. Talk about a paradigm shift!

One of my major businesses growing up was my guitar-teaching business. When I was sixteen years old, a yellow flyer appeared in my mailbox that said, "Make money teaching music lessons." The flyer advertised that positions were available for piano, guitar, voice, and drums. My mother had force-fed me piano lessons from age three until age fourteen and I hated the piano with a passion, so I wasn't interested in me teaching that. My guitar playing was primitive at best, my voice was terrible, and I couldn't play drums, but I was a very good bass player and bass was almost the same as guitar.

When I saw the flyer, it ignited an idea, and I thought about it and figured that bass was similar enough to the guitar so I applied for the guitar-teaching job. Of course I was hired! The company that hired me was more like an agency that would locate music students, sign them up to a program, and then subcontract the teaching out to me, and they immediately sent four students.

At the age of sixteen, I began teaching guitar students out of my parent's basement. I started practicing and educating myself to become a better guitar player (one of the traits of entrepreneurs—learn, be a self-starter, and make it happen) so that I could stay ahead of my students. I didn't wait until I knew how to play guitar at a high level to start. I jumped in and started teaching kids, and at night I would have to teach myself all at the same time.

When I was seventeen, my parents separated and I moved in with my mother. I took my guitar-teaching business with me and as I went to school at the university, I taught lessons to children, teenagers, and adults out of my mother's living room. It developed into a strong little student business, something that I could always count on for income, and I became really good at teaching.

I resented the fact that the agency who hired me took nearly half of the money that was being billed out to the students, so I began to teach my own students as well as my own. I called the agency a few times to negotiate a better wage, but they warned me that if I raised my wage, they would raise their price and I would get fewer students. There seemed to be a balance between the quantity of customers I would have and the price I could charge.

Very quickly I was introduced to the law of supply and demand. A higher price set for teenage guitar lessons will typically equate to a lower demand for the same lessons.

If I charged more, I would have fewer customers, and if I charged less, I would be busier. I decided that I would still take the students from the agency at the "half price" rate that I was receiving after they took their cut, but in the end I built up my business out of client referrals, which allowed me to charge full price.

This lesson of working for an agency made me realize the importance of having distribution. I was able to sell my time to the agency at a wholesale price and because I had traffic, I was able to capture some "full price" retail customers as well. As a student, I was living the dream. I could cram all of my students into less than 12 hours per week and I was earning a clear $1,000 per month without leaving my mother's home. I enjoyed the work I was doing and I loved the freedom that I could afford. It was my first taste of earning money on my terms with minimal time investment.

Entrepreneurs learn as they go. They tend to be the kind of people who can easily adapt and accomplish a lot, without a whole lot of stress or planning. They approach an opportunity head on and are focused on making it happen despite any limitations.

Before my successful venture as a guitar teacher, I had worked for Tim Horton's, a large Canadian coffee chain that sold drugs, aka: addictive coffee and donuts to Canadians. I can still remember my job interview and agreeing to work for the minimum wage allowed at the time: $6.50 per hour. I smiled and fumbled my way through my first corporate job interview and at the end, the manager across the table offered me a job.

I was so excited to have passed the interview that I was ready to accept any number of hours or any terms. The manager offered me a 25-cent premium on my wage if I agreed to work the graveyard shift from dusk until dawn. Since it was summer, and since I had nothing to do during the day anyways, I happily agreed to the 25-cent rise.

When I got home, I told my parents that I had got a summer job like they had told me to. I was excited to tell them that I was making 25 cents over minimum wage because I agreed to the night shift.

"No, no, no," my father said. "You can't work the night shift; you need at least $15 an hour to do that."

"But Dad!" I exclaimed. "How can they afford to pay me $15 an hour in the middle of the night? Not that many people are buying donuts and coffee at the shop at 2 a.m.!"

"Working in the middle of the night is dangerous," he said. "What if someone robs the store? I won't have you working those hours, so go back to them and tell them that you can't work those hours!"

It was an order, and not a request.

My father, although he was an entrepreneur, had socialist values that the workers should do less and get paid more. As a teenager, I was OK with minimum wage, and I was even OK with the 25-cent premium.

The next day I arrived at work and told my manager that I couldn't work the night shift because my parents wouldn't allow it. He was furious and told me that he had hired me on the premise of working the night shift, and now he had to find someone else. Although I had angered him, I wasn't fired. Instead, I was just given fewer shifts and threw my 25-cent premium out the window.

Working at $6.50 per hour at Tim Horton's was difficult work, low pay, and the customers did not appreciate me much as I served them. My co-workers who served coffee and donuts with me were mostly single moms, retired people who lived below the poverty line, refugees from war-torn Afghanistan, and other teenagers like me. I wondered how these people could afford to ride the bus across town to work, pay for rent, put food on the table, feed the kids, and pay all of the other bills to stay alive. I could see that working a minimum wage life was brutal for these people, as they would need to take on extra shifts to survive.

When I became a guitar teacher, I was now a skilled worker with knowledge, and I charged $32 per hour, which was nearly five times the earnings of my coffee shop wage! My time was worth only $6.50 at the time in that economy, but because I had leveraged my knowledge of music, I was able to command $32 per hour, which allowed me to provide more value while earning more and working less. The contrast of the two jobs taught me a very valuable lesson that an investment in knowledge was going to be the most important investment I could ever make and one that would later be my ticket out of a poverty life.

25 PAY CHECKS EVERY MONTH

How many checks do you deposit into your bank account each month? Is it one on the first and another on the fifteenth? Most people have two paycheck deposits from the corporation they work for, but an entrepreneur has many more. The more customers, the more deposits. The more prospects in your sales funnel, the more potential you have to increase those deposits.

As a guitar teacher, I no longer had a boss like I did at my minimum-wage job. Instead, I had customers. Having customers made me feel free and secure in the world because I realized that if I lost one customer, I would have more to replace them.

When you are an entrepreneur and you have customers (instead of having a boss or just a job), you have freedom. One lost customer can be replaced by another.

When I had my donut and coffee job, if my boss didn't like me, I would be fired. By getting fired I would lose my one and only customer. When I started my guitar business, a diverse customer base meant that I was achieving security and freedom all at the same time.

Over time I grew my small part-time business from 4 to 25 recurring customers, and every month I would take 25 handwritten personal checks to the bank rather than two biweekly paychecks that most employees make. Some months I would lose a customer or two, other months I would gain extra customers, so my income fluctuated a little bit, but I was fine by the fluctuations. For stability I kept my expenses low, my savings high, and I loved the freedom of not having to answer to a boss or a corporate structure. The freedom was exciting, yet I felt secure in that I could predict my monthly income with relative ease.

Every month I would take my 25 checks into the bank and smile at the teller as she would organize them, sort them, stamp them, and deposit them into my account. Since I had hardly any expenses, I was able to clear a tidy $1,000 profit each month. For most people $1,000 a month is on the poverty line, but for a young kid with very few expenses, it was all the money in the world. I was learning how to be an entrepreneur and enthusiastic about saving cash at the same time.

To clear $1,000 cash a month was like working 40 hours a week full-time at my minimum-wage job, but I was only working 8-12 hours a week from the comfort of my own home. I had no car, no cell phone, no gas, no commute, no employees, no advertising, no marketing, and was making pure profit. As far as I was concerned, I had a pretty good little business, except the only downside was if I wanted more money, I had to sell more of my time and I could never leave town to go on a trip because I had to teach guitar lessons scattered throughout the week. Other than that, I was happy.

Hope is for the hopeless and happiness is fleeting. As time went on, I started to feel content and lazy. My mind started to numb with doing the same routine over and over again. Although I was making money, my ambition was starting to roar and I became dissatisfied with my position in life. I didn't want to spend the rest of my life living in my mother's living room, teaching guitar lessons to teenage boys who wanted to capture the hearts and minds of teenage girls.

I started to consider my situation and knew that I had to change something. I had recently read *Rich Dad Poor Dad* and it said that if you wanted to make money in real estate or learn to invest in real estate, you had to educate yourself first. I understood the need for education because education had been the difference between lifting me out of the poverty cycle of minimum wage and up to a living wage as a guitar teacher. I also understood that I wanted to have a better lifestyle and wanted money to go on trips and own a car and a home. I certainly didn't want to be poor or live a modest lifestyle. My spirit was too big.

The freedom I had carved out for myself slowly became a prison as I began to think of the greener grass and the bigger world outside of my micro empire.

One of the hallmarks of successful entrepreneurs is angst. Entrepreneurs are often idea factories, igniters, and visionaries. They feel bored or anxious if they're at a stalemate, or when they're not DOING.

I decided that I would break out of my comfort zone and become educated in real estate and investing. Teaching guitar was far too limited and it was time to uproot my efforts and make my fortune in a completely different industry. The decision to change was painful and scary to think about: I had invested my entire life into music and now it was time to throw it all away.

Like an immigrant preparing to leave his homeland and move to a brand-new country, I looked at my monthly budget and began to cut out every expense. I was able to save 70% of my income for my future real-estate education and I cut out all expenditures except for the bare necessities. Most people would cringe at cutting their budgets down all the way, but I was energized by the thought of escaping the desert island I was trapped on. In my heart, I knew that the only way that I was going to escape my dead-end situation was preparing diligently and by saving all of my resources for the journey off the island. My entertainment budget went down to $20 a week and that included eating out. My once-a-week treat was a toasted, buttered bagel from Tim Horton's that I would buy for $1 and eat on the bus to and from university. I was determined to invest all of my free cash into real estate and become rich or smash up on the rocks as a failure.

SELF MADE LESSONS

1. Immigrants are four times more likely to become millionaires than native-born Americans.

2. The best opportunities always come when you aren't ready for them. Sacrifice something and seize them anyways!

3. Knowledge is your best leverage to escape poverty. With an investment in a music education I was able to charge more than five times minimum wage because I had specialized knowledge.

4. Having 25 customers is more secure than having one customer, aka: a boss and a job. You can lose one or two customers and still stay in business. But if you lose your job as an employee, you lose 100% of your customers.

5. A thousand dollars a month of clear profit in a small side business can be equivalent to the net profit made at a real job after expenses like a car, work clothes, eating out for lunch, and taxes. Sometimes making more money isn't the answer. It's not about how much money you make, it's about how much money you keep!

Visit SelfMadeConfessions.com for more lessons.

Confession #7

"YOU COULD BE DEALING DRUGS FOR ALL WE KNOW"

"Banks have a new image. Now you have 'a friend,'
your friendly banker. If the banks are so friendly,
how come they chain down the pens?"

ALAN KING

Successful people are always learning. I like to call learning mindfeeding or feeding of the mind and it can be done through online education, seminars, or time learning from mentors and coaches. Sometimes mindfeeding could be by reading, enrolling in classes, or intense self-study. The most successful people in the world mindfeed every day.

When I decided to enter the world of real estate, my mind was starving and was ready to be fed! I wasn't going to leave anything up to chance, and I decided to start devouring everything I could find on money, real estate, and investing.

I followed the rules of credit that the banker shared with me, and continued to buy things on my credit card.

I had started to build my credit up with small food purchases such as Coke, chips, and bagels on my $500 limit credit card. I felt as though I had built credit and decided to apply for a mortgage again through my local bank after being rejected the first time. I waited in line to meet with my banker and we sat down in the same chairs we had sat in the first time I applied for credit.

"You're making your payments every month on time. Very good!" said the banker. Although he was a banker, he sounded more like a doctor.

"I want to take out a mortgage to buy cash-flowing investment real estate!" I said, excited with my progress. "I'm making good money every month, and you can see that I have more savings and cash... I'm ready to buy a property!"

"You're right," said the banker, "you do have cash, and you are making money. Every month you are depositing a similar amount of funds into your account. But we have a problem..."

"What's the problem?" I asked, getting worried.

"We don't know where your money is coming from. You could be dealing drugs for all we know... we don't know if the money you are bringing in is actually yours! Do you have a paystub from your employer?"

"No, I don't have a paystub from my employer! I'm self-employed! You know that! I have customers from my small business. I don't have any paperwork!" I was beginning to get frustrated.

The banker leaned back in the chair. "Well, if you are self-employed, we need two years of tax returns to verify your income and then we can continue this conversation about getting a mortgage for an investment property."

"I haven't been in business long enough," I almost yelled, frustrated. "What can I do?" I began to feel desperate.

The banker stood and began to usher me out of his office. "Nothing," he replied bluntly. "Go get a job, file your taxes, and come back in a few years."

Defeated, I walked home to my mother's house instead of taking the bus. I thought about how difficult it was for me to get the credibility to buy my first property. The bank wanted me to build my credit, so I did. The bank wanted my income, so I showed it to them. The bank wanted cash for a down payment and I had it. Although I had cash and cash flow, I didn't have credit and was missing a major piece of the investment property puzzle.

When I got home, I leafed through the property listings in the real-estate news and grabbed a black Sharpie marker and began to mark the uninteresting properties with an X and circle the moneymakers with an O. I lay on the couch in my mother's living room and as I finished getting through the entire magazine of listings, my mother arrived home from work.

I thought to myself, my mother has a job, and my mother has credit. Maybe my mother can help me get a mortgage, and perhaps she can co-sign and then I can provide the cash to buy the property and pay for any expenses that may come up. I thought the venture sounded like a good idea, so I got off the couch and met her in the kitchen as she was unpacking groceries.

"Mom, I want to buy a cash-flowing rental property. I want to make more money, but the bank won't give me a mortgage"

My mother looked at me. "That's nice, dear."

"The bank says I don't have any credit because I don't have a real job... and I need someone to help me out. I need someone to cosign... who can let me use their credit to buy property so that I can... make more money." My pitch was disorganized and poorly delivered. I was nervous and wasn't sure how my mother would react.

"Mom, will you help me get a mortgage and cosign for me?" I looked her in the eyes and we both froze for a moment. I could see pain in her face and then she turned away. My pitch triggered something inside of her.

"That's what your father always wanted," she said. "He always wanted to buy investment property and needed me to cosign at the bank. Ever since we separated, I've been stuck and attached to his business lines of credit and I don't want anything to do with you or your mortgages. I will not sign anything; you're starting to remind me of your father!"

Her words were a mortal blow to my confidence. If I had been a hot air balloon buoyant on enthusiasm, her words pierced through me, and my confidence came crashing down to the floor. I couldn't believe the effect that her lack of confidence had on me. I couldn't believe that she would compare my ambitions and dreams to the failed ventures of my father and I felt as though all of her support over the years had been yanked away from me in an instant.

I left her in the kitchen and went upstairs to my room to stare at the ceiling and come up with a new plan for getting my first deal done.

SELF MADE LESSONS

1. A strong income is not enough to buy get a mortgage. The bank wants to know where your money comes from and they want to verify it!

2. If you have no credit, get someone else to provide the credit to buy a property.

Visit <u>SelfMadeConfessions.com</u> for more lessons.

Confession #8

GET A JOB TO GO INTO $50,000 OF CREDIT CARD DEBT

"Choose a job you love, and you will never
have to work a day in your life."

<small>CONFUCIUS</small>

I thought I was smarter than everyone else and I thought I was special. When I had my rock band, I thought I could become a rock star without paying my dues. I thought I could somehow bypass years of touring and playing empty bars to become successful. Perhaps I had just watched too much television. When I decided I wanted to become wealthy through real estate, I made the same mistake and thought that I could jump straight into self-employment and skip the step of having a real job with a paystub.

I had the flawed lottery thinking that I could get something for nothing and that somehow I could flip a switch and become a millionaire overnight. Unfortunately, in reality, something for nothing doesn't exist… or maybe I just couldn't flip the millionaire switch in time. Either way, I was back to the well-worn path of trying to find a job that would satisfy my short-term needs for money and help me take out mortgages from the bank. I wanted something brainless and mindless so I could sell my body eight hours a day but still keep my mind and my soul. I wanted to put in the minimum and take out the maximum. I was motivated purely by money and nothing else. I believed that I was selling out and working for the man rather than working for myself. In many ways I broke one of the most important rules of money, which is "work to learn, not to earn."

Very simply, I was seeking to get a stable day job for proven cash, and work on my real-estate business at night.

Through a friend, I found the perfect job that fit all of my criteria. I took a job working for Frito-Lay, the company that makes Doritos, Lays chips, Cheetos, and other well-known brands of salted snacks. As a good entrepreneur I had found arbitrage in the market. Arbitrage is where something can be bought at a low price and instantly sold at a slightly higher price. Frito-Lay was offering $17 per hour to mindlessly put chips on shelves every morning at 4 a.m. while the same employees at Wal-Mart were earning $8 per hour to perform the exact same task. The brilliance of taking the job at Frito Lay was that I was performing an $8-per-hour task and getting paid $17 per hour on a guaranteed salary. With a guaranteed salary, the bank would approve me for a mortgage. In one move, my credit problems were solved and because my shift at Frito-Lay started at 4 a.m. and ended at noon, I still had five business hours every day to make money in real estate and guitar teaching.

I began the brutal immigrant lifestyle of waking up at 3 a.m. to start work at Frito-Lay at 4 a.m. Every day I would be done work at noon, then I would work on my real-estate deals for five hours until 5 p.m. In the evening, I would teach guitar for two hours and then work on another side business for two hours until I fell asleep.

Everyday, I woke up and chased value until I dropped dead at night. This insane death march continued for six months until I nearly collapsed.

Being a salaried worker had many benefits though, especially when it came to banking, mortgages, credit cards, and borrowing money. Since my employer paid me a salary every two weeks, suddenly, as if by magic, all of the banks wanted to lend to me. As a credit-starved and cash-poor entrepreneur, I made the most of my salary and leveraged it to the max. Every few months I would call upon all of the bank and apply for lines of credit, credit cards, term loans, car loans, RRSP loans, student loans, and any other type of loans they would give me. My friends and I called it a "credit blitz" where blitz is the German word for lightning. I would call all of the credit card companies in one afternoon and apply for the maximum credit possible. I would ask for $10,000, $20,000, or even $50,000 credit limit increases on my credit cards and since I called all of the companies at once, many of them would not know about my other applications and approve me. Although my salary was only around $35,000 per year, I was able to get more than $50,000 of unsecured credit to buy anything I wanted!

I started my blitz with the cheapest product, like student lines of credit, which would be easy to get at $10,000 a piece. At the time, these lines had an unbelievably low interest rate of 3%, which was pretty much free money! I was young, fresh out of school, and learned that if I registered for a few extra classes, applied for student credit, and then dropped the classes after receiving the credit products, I qualified for cheap-as-free money. I exploited student credit as much as I could and even used it to speculate on commodities. With one $10,000 student line of credit, I maxed it out twice on silver bullion and managed to double my money twice!

After the banks caught on that I was no longer a student, I switched to personal lines of credit, which were not nearly as much fun. These lines of credit were painful to apply for and came in increments of $10,000 as well. I had a few of them, but they were at interest rates of 7–10% and were much more expensive to use. The other problem with the personal lines of credit was because they were unsecured, the banks would see these credit products as risky and I would often be asked to close my lines. For some reason the bank saw no issue with giving me irresponsible amounts of credit card credit, but they defended and took away my unsecured lines of credit almost as soon as they issued them.

Eventually, I became tired of lines of credit and switched to the holy grail of seed capital for small entrepreneurs—credit cards. Credit cards had always been evil to me as I was raised on a "cash only" mentality and debt was evil, but when I started to learn how to use credit cards profitably, I became hooked like a drug addict. Credit cards are the most risky credit products for the banks and were also the most aggressive at marketing themselves to me. I applied for a credit card at every bank and eventually, my mailbox was full of credit card offers for 0.00% for six months, 0.9% for six months, or 1.99% for six months. I noticed a reversal in the mentality of credit card lenders, because these cards lent money at higher rates of interest, around 19.99%. They wanted my business more than I wanted theirs. The problem was that 19.99% was expensive money and

I didn't want to use it to invest in property. However, I learned that if I called the credit card company and negotiated a lower rate, they would give me the same credit at 8–12%, which was very reasonable, even attractive compared with my lines of credit, which the bankers would close if they saw me as a risk.

For some reason, the bankers never cared about my credit card balances and I was never asked to close my credit card accounts. The lines of credit were always under attack from various bankers and they would request that I close them. However, I could have a huge amount of available credit cards and the bankers didn't seem to care.

When I started at Frito-Lay, I had only $500 of available credit on one card. By the time I quit my job, I had access to more than $50,000 of credit card money at 10.99% and over $800,000 of personal mortgages on rental properties. I had leveraged my small living salary to the max and had borrowed the maximum I could from my future labor at that job. That $50,000 of seed capital that I would borrow and pay off over and over again became the base of my power in the property market. I used those cards for everything from purchasing property, renovating property, hiring coaches and mentors, travel, marketing, advertising, and even basic survival during lean times. The house of cards that I built on credit eventually became the base of working capital for my small empire. Years later when I no longer needed them, I paid them off and froze my cards in a block of ice in the freezer. The cards served me well in building a property empire, and I would never cut up my cards or throw away my credit, but I froze them so that I could return to my "all cash" mentality and save my credit for the deal of the century.

When I had maxed out my potential credit cards, lines of credit, mortgages, and anything else I could get my hands on, it was time to quit my job. My job had served its purpose as a vehicle to obtain the credit needed to start my business, but I knew that staying with my low salary forever would kill my spirit.

My time with personal credit was done, I was maxed, and I couldn't get any more credit cards or any more mortgages. The only way I could borrow more money was through bringing on partners and using other people's credit. It was time to take my business to the next level.

SELF MADE CONFESSIONS

1. Never take a job just for the money. Always work to learn, not to earn!

2. One of the fastest ways to get ahead is to have two jobs. One to earn a living, and the second to get ahead. Another bonus of having two jobs is that you are too busy to waste your extra cash.

3. Student credit is some of the cheapest and easiest credit you will ever obtain.

4. You can use student loans to buy anything you want, even investments!

5. Credit cards are often used as seed capital by entrepreneurs to start businesses with little or no money.

6. Credit cards are good to start a business, but as soon as you can, pay them off and freeze them in the freezer. It's very easy to get carried away with cheap, easy credit.

Visit <u>SelfMadeConfessions.com</u> for more lessons.

Confession #9

YOUR FIRST INVESTMENT WILL SUCK

"Work like a slave, command like a king, create like a God."

CONSTANTIN BRANCUSI

Good entrepreneurs put their money to work. Great entrepreneurs place their money into slave labor. A smart entrepreneur will have all of his money working at all times, but unfortunately, every entrepreneur has dreams that are bigger than his wallet will allow.

Consequently, most entrepreneurs are obsessed with making their money work hard and are perpetually out of cash. As a young man with big dreams and virtually no cash, I was the perfect candidate for going into business for myself. From a very young age, I had to learn the two major skills of the entrepreneur: 1) operating with no money and 2) investing other people's money wisely.

Although I eventually learned how to operate with no money and invest other people's money efficiently, my first investment was a dud. When I was sixteen years old, I worked for a summer at a diner. The diner was a small mom-and-pop diner where I scraped egg yolks off plates and cooked burgers for tourists. My wage was $5.75 per hour and every day for a whole summer I worked a split shift of 4 hours on, 4 hours off, followed by another 4 hours of work.

The days were long, the pay was low, but at the end of the summer I had saved a clean $1,000 profit. At the advice of my grandmother, I decided that I was "going to invest" my profits to earn a return.

Grandma took me to my neighborhood bank, where I approached the bank teller and told her I "wanted to invest." The very pretty and very persuasive bank teller showed me a chart of returns and explained that if I locked in my money into a guaranteed investment, I would earn a handsome sum of 1.4% at the end of the year and would be much richer than the year before.

I was no genius, but felt a sick feeling when I calculated that I would only make $14 on my hard earned $1,000 and I thought about what my grandmother and father had told me about interest. They promised me that at some point in my life, I would be able to live off of the interest earned on my investments. A mere $14 seemed pathetically low for my $1,000, but Grandma smiled at me and assured me that my investment with the bank was sound.

One year later, when I pulled my $1,000 out of the bank and took my $14 profit on my investment, I read the statement on my checking account and it stated that if I kept a $1,000 minimum in my checking account, then I would pay $0 in monthly banking fees. Since I had left my $1,000 in a guaranteed investment at 1.4% with the bank, I had paid $4 per month in checking fees, which totaled $48 for the year while only earning $14 from my investment. I am no math genius, but when my investment is earning me $14 annually and costing me $48 in fees, it is time to stop investing. My first investment of my life netted me a loss of $34. The bank had robbed me.

> *"The best way to rob a bank is to own one."*
>
> WILLIAM K BLACK

As I reviewed my statement, I felt the pain of loss and it became very clear that investing with the bank was not the way that the rich invested. I knew that there was money to be made through investment, just not with guaranteed investments at the bank.

I was always entrepreneurial in my endeavors, but I hadn't earned my stripes as an entrepreneur quite yet. I always aspired to work for myself and knew that there was "no job like no job."

"No job" for most of the year as a teenager meant that when I did make money on one of my entrepreneurial schemes, I had to hide the cash and stay liquid in case I needed it. I developed an all-cash mentality and carried absolutely no debt, but when my dreams started to get bigger than my cash, I began to realize that I would never have enough.

When I was a guitar teacher wanting to become a real-estate entrepreneur, I saved 70% of my income and realized that I would never have enough. My annual income was only $10,000 per year and even if I saved 70% of it, that was only $7,000, which was certainly not enough to fund dreams as big as mine.

If I invested my $7,000 of savings into the bank at 1.4% like Grandma had told me to years ago, I would only earn $98 in an entire year.

Even if I invested it at a rate of return of 100% per year, a $7,000 profit still wasn't big enough to fund my dreams. I knew that investing my own cash into investments would never solve my problems, so I looked for other ways of investing my personal money.

"I think that much of the advice given to young men about saving money is wrong. I never saved a cent until I was forty years old. I invested in myself."

HENRY FORD

I knew I would never have enough money, no matter how hard I worked, so I looked for avenues that would grow my income in exponential ways. The #1 way that I found to grow my income was to invest in education.

Years ago when I became a guitar teacher and started earning $32 per hour instead of $6, I had been able to leverage my earnings by learning about music and teaching my knowledge to others.

One of my first and most important investments in myself was a $1,500 real-estate weekend where I would begin to understand that I could make $10,000, $20,000, or $30,000 per deal in real estate multiple times per year. What made this information even better was that I could earn this kind of income with none of my own money or credit.

If I only made $10,000 extra from real estate in a year with my new $1,500 knowledge once, that would be a 666% annual return on my $1,500 investment. If I was able to make an extra $10,000 per year for the next 75 years of my life, then that would be a 50,000% increase on my money over my life.

By doing this kind of math, I quickly learned that my dollars, my money, was reserved for my education and that I would use other people's money for my deals, businesses, and investments. I would pay out 8%, 10%, 12%, or even 20% out to my investors, but because I would invest none of my own money, I would make an infinite return on money that was never mine in the first place.

Although the first investment of my life was a flop, my second investment turned out to be a wild success. When I was 21, I began promoting rock'n'roll shows that my band would play at. Initially, my promoter business was a huge failure. I was blinded by my love and passion for music—and because of my blindness, I made stupid business errors. Every show I booked lost money because I took on all of the risk and hoped that the market would somehow favor me.

Just like a bad real-estate investor, I sank my own money into the venture: $500 into renting a hall for my little rock show. I also rented lights, a PA system, printed posters, and tickets and found volunteers to work the show. I would then get on the phone and invite some of my friends' bands to come play and hopefully sell tickets. Like clockwork, every single show would run empty, the bands I chose to play would be too lazy to promote the show, and because there was no promotion, I would fail to make any ticket sales at the door. Nearly every show I promoted would run empty and I would lose nearly $500 on my passion. The madness of losing $500 over and over again persisted for some time until I decided to go bigger. There was a bigger venue that was $1,000 to rent and I clearly couldn't afford it, I didn't have the money to rent it, and I was scared of taking on the risk of a show that was over $1,000 to put on. So I booked the $1,000 venue in advance and would pay only a $100 deposit toward my future booking.

Once I had the date booked, I would call the same bands that played my money-losing shows and I would sell them each a wholesale block of tickets for $300. I would book four bands at $300 a block and before the show had even started I would make $1200 in revenue and I would have only $100 of my own money invested into the venture.

To make my business model even better, because the other bands had paid to play, they had skin in the game and they all promoted and sold their tickets to their fans and I took the extra door sales. I also made money on my own band's sales and the merchandise sales from the back of the room. I was able to repeat this process over and over again and while in university, the shows would profit $1,000 every time with absolutely no risk.

By changing my business model and tweaking a few details, I had gone from losing $500 every show to making $1,000 every show and the major difference was leverage.

I had learned how to leverage $100 into a $1,000 venue and because the value of the show was higher, other bands were willing and begging me to pay $300 for a spot at a $1,000 venue.

This concept of leverage seduced my mind and I began to obsess over property because I could buy a $100,000 house with only $10,000 or 10% in the same way that I could buy a $1,000 venue with only $100 or 10%. The leverage and increase in value from shows I could afford to shows I could never afford was the difference in my development and transformed my mind from a money-losing mind to a money-making mind.

REAL-LIFE LESSONS FROM THIS CONFESSION

1. Guaranteed investments at the bank return yields so low that they don't even beat inflation. If you invest in these, you are losing purchasing power to inflation.

2. The best way to rob a bank is to own one.

3. No matter how much cash you accumulate or save, you will never have enough.

4. Investments into your education and self-development will always

outpace investments made into anything else (WARNING: only if you apply your education).

5. Use your money for your education and other people's money for your investments

6. Avoid investing in businesses of passion. You will be blinded by passion and will fail to make rational investments.

7. Learn to use leverage: You make more money on ventures you can't afford than on ventures you can afford. Use your $100 to book a $1,000 venue. Or use your $10,000 to buy a $100,000 property.

8. A money-losing venture and a money-making venture are often very similar, except for a few minor differences. Success and failure are closer than you think.

9. Don't be afraid to fail. The formula for success is to take your current rate of failure and double it!

Visit <u>SelfMadeConfessions.com</u> for more lessons.

Confession #10

IF YOU WANT TO BE RICH, WORK FOR FREE

"Don't be addicted to money. Work to learn.
Don't work for money. Work for knowledge."

ROBERT KIYOSAKI

I had been on my quest to buy an investment property for months and was starting to feel as though my efforts were in vain. I bought the books; I read everything I could find. I attended all of the classes I could afford, and even some classes I couldn't afford! My ambition and craving for knowledge was beginning to outweigh my income.

Slowly but surely I was taking on debt to attend seminar after seminar. At the time, I was only earning $10,000 a year by teaching guitar in my mother's living room. Very quickly after becoming a seminar junkie, I had put myself into an entire year's income of debt. The credit cards that I had responsibly ordered to build credit had suddenly become maxed and I was moving in the wrong direction.

At this point, most sane people would quit and decide that real estate wasn't for them. But for myself, I felt that my debt was justified. Although I had lost all my cash and was one year's earnings in the hole, I kept going. They say that when a business isn't doing well, it's time to spend money. Somehow I was going to spend my way out of my situation. I bought: $197 weekends, $347 weekends, $497 weekends, $1,500 weekends, a $3,000 weekend, and finally a $7,000 one-week seminar. I felt like my head was going to burst with random facts about real estate, business plans, cash-flow statements, and all other sorts of information I could not apply.

I was still a property virgin; I still hadn't "done it." I always felt that there was one more thing I needed to know and that one more thing always came with a price tag—a price tag that I always paid. I had become addicted to paying the price tag and studying the materials but never following through.

This addiction got worse and worse until a miracle happened—I maxed out all of my credit. I no longer had any more cash or credit to spend on courses and I felt flurry of emotions while reviewing my credit card statements that began to show up in the mail. Every single card was maxed and the interest rates were high, at 19.99%. I had begun my seminar spree with $5,000 of earned cash in the bank and absolutely zero debt. Within a few months of feeding my addiction, I was now $10,000 in credit card debt and had zero cash in the bank. I might as well have been doing hard drugs because my money evaporated nearly as quickly as if I had been a heroin or cocaine addict. In truth, my brain was high on the thoughts of getting rich and the piles of money I could make in real estate.

On Wall Street, stockbrokers get addicted to cocaine because the rush of the drug is identical to the rush of making money. I was no different—a junkie, an addict, and it was time to cut my addiction and go cold turkey. When an addict goes off drugs completely, they shiver and sweat. They vomit out the toxins absorbed into their flesh and undergo a very painful process. I didn't vomit, but I did lie on my bed in the fetal position feeling helpless and beginning to regret my choices.

A man becomes poor when he wants things he does not have. A man also becomes poor the moment he desires things he cannot afford.

My prolonged desire of wanting that which I did not have drained all of the cash out of my bank account. Through my greed, I sank into debt and mortgaged my future. I used to love the freedom of making $10,000 a year in my mother's living room and not having to work because I had no debt. That $10,000 was mine; there was no one else to pay. Instead, I had sold my freedom and now woke up every morning running from lions, just like everyone else with debt. The feeling was awful and I felt tricked. I had no more money, no more credit, and had to change my ways, but I had an addiction, so I did what most addicts do: I began to look for my fix in any way I could.

Like a homeless man who scavenges for cigarette butts out of the trash, I began to hunt for free events. I was hungry for any shred or morsel of information that would bring me to the promised land of riches in real estate.

I would slither from hotel basement to hotel basement, trying to get my fix of free real-estate information. I was like a bottom-feeding leech looking for the blood of a host that I could live off. The problem with my strategy was all of the free information I had already heard.

There were many seminars coming in and out of town, and they all offered the same rudimentary information that I already knew, and the people attending were the same seminar junkies that met late at night in basements around town, trying to cure their fears and weaknesses with camaraderie.

One afternoon I got an unexpected call on my mother's landline. I was home, reading on the couch when the phone rang; it was Tony. "Hey, Stefan, how are you?" Tony asked in his dry, analytical voice. Tony's tone of voice always sounded patronizing, like he didn't care about you when he was talking to you. He was really a sweet and genuine guy; it just came off the wrong way.

"I'm doing good; what's up?" I answered the phone almost rudely; I was weaning off my addiction to money and didn't care to talk about feelings.

"I'm doing good," he said, as if he was reading off a script. "Hey, Stefan, I want to invite you out to an event that we are putting on in town and it's free, and I thought of you, and thought you would like to come and check it out this weekend." Tony's words were dry in tone and sounded robotic like a bad telemarketer, but we had built up a bond driving across the country, so I knew that he was just really bad on the phone.

"Great, I'll be there."

I scribbled down some notes about the time and location and hung up. I was officially the homeless man collecting cigarette butts.

The day of the event came and I was wearing my long black trench coat. My hair was long, and I had on oversized studio headphones that I wore on the bus to listen to rock'n'roll. My ex-lover (rock'n'roll) and I had ridden the bus across town with two bus transfers to make the 7 p.m. seminar. The times advertised were convenient for anyone who was broke and wanted a way out. There were two options—noon and 7 p.m. I opted for 7 p.m. It was 2008 and the stock market had just crashed, real estate in the USA was taking a nosedive, and people were scared. As a brilliant marketing move, this seminar was called "Get Rich in Canada" and was packed with a line-up waiting outside.

The room was full of faces that had been kissed by fear. There were baby boomers, echo boomers, Generation Xers, and old people who should have been retired. All were fighting for seats.

Somehow the fear in the economy had shaken up every dormant, complacent investor in the market and blood was flowing through the streets. I would later learn that some of these investors were bleeding profusely and had recently lost 30%, 40%, or 50% of their portfolios in the stock market and the panic had caused uproar.

The people in the seminar room were terrified, broken, and bleeding.

Many of them feared that the sky was finally falling and that financial Armageddon was upon them. They wanted answers to their fears as they rallied around a shared pain. They were looking for someone to lead them out of the bloodbath—they were looking for a messiah.

The room quieted down and the speaker took the stage. He was in his early forties, and an average-looking man with an average build, an average haircut, an average suit, and a deep, smooth voice that could charm the wallet out of your pocket.

The speaker spoke for 3 hours about how we had been tricked: the banks had become rich at our expense. He used common language and was very down to earth. The room slowly relaxed as the speaker calmed their fears with a sweet venom. His words were like warm honey dripping from his mouth and the smooth delivery sedated the audience.

"If you want to be rich, work for free," he said partway through his presentation. My ears perked up at this piece of wisdom. I had $10,000 of debt and hardly any cash to my name. I could no longer afford to pay for my real-estate tuition with money, so working for free sounded good to me.

The speaker pulled a young man in his twenties onstage and asked him in front of the audience, "Can you work for free?".

"No!" the young man nervously replied. "My dad says I need to get paid at least ten dollars an hour or I need to go join a good union if I'm going to work."

"Wrong answer!" said the speaker. "That's why you aren't rich."

The speaker then asked if there were any real-estate investors in the room, and many eager hands shot up. The speaker selected a man in his fifties and brought him onstage too. "You invest in real estate, right?" the speaker asked.

"Yes," the man replied.

"And how many rental properties do you have?"

"I have twenty," he replied proudly.

"Do you need some free help to collect rents, clean the houses, clean the gutters, mow the lawns, and do other odd jobs around the houses?" asked the speaker.

"Oh yes, I would love to have some help."

The speaker then turned to the man in his twenties and said, "If you work for free for this man with twenty houses, you will do some odd jobs, but you will learn about real estate and how to make money. Can you work for free for him?"

The young man paused and the audience could see that he was learning his lesson. "Yes," the young man replied, slowly smiling and letting the message sink in.

The audience gave a roaring applause as if a Super Bowl touchdown had been scored. Underneath the deafening applause, I learned a major principle of wealth: "work to learn, not to earn."

As I sat in my seat and reflected on the lesson that had unfolded in front of me, I began to see the connection between theory and practice. I felt foolish for spending thousands of dollars on seminars. Why didn't I find a mentor and offer to work for free instead?

The real knowledge was waiting for me, along with great riches, if I would volunteer myself to work for free and become an apprentice for one benevolent master. It dawned on me that humanity has always learned with a master-apprentice style education system. In the old days, if you wanted to be a blacksmith, you would live and work with a blacksmith for free until you became a master.

I knew this educational concept as a musician. In music, I had a mentor and I would pay him to teach me as well as volunteer for him and do whatever was required to "pay my dues" in the industry. Somehow I forgot about the way that the world really worked and the artificial system of university and high school had conditioned me to take classes rather than seek mentors and masters to offer my free labor.

As the seminar ended and the room began to vacate, I waited until I was finally alone with the speaker. I held my breath and my palms sweated as I approached him, looked him in the eyes, and said, "I want to work for free."

SELF MADE LESSONS

1. The education you can't afford is the one that makes you rich.

2. If you want to be rich, work for free. Find a mentor with more experience and offer to work for free.

3. Although seminars are powerful, don't get carried away by becoming a junkie.

4. Remember: work to learn, not to earn.

Visit SelfMadeConfessions.com for more lessons.

Confession #11

OPPORTUNITY IS HIDDEN
IN PLAIN SIGHT

"Opportunity is missed by most people because
it is dressed in overalls and looks like work."

THOMAS A. EDISON

"I want to work for free" was my pitch: cold, no frills, and direct. I was like a wild beast that had just been violently tamed. Although I had a fighting spirit screaming at me not to submit to this man, I swallowed my pride and stared into the speaker's eyes as I waited for his response.

It's sometimes startling to see that a life-changing lesson can be handed to a room of 400 people on a silver platter and I was the only one out of the group who stayed behind to work for free. It's ironic that we go searching for wealth—while wealth, riches, and opportunity are hidden in plain sight.

The speaker smiled at my request and said, "OK, talk to Tony and I'll see you next time I'm in town." That was it; no rebuttal, no objection. I was expecting him to resist.

Tony was my connection to this speaker and the source of knowledge that I deeply desired. At this point, because of my connection, working for free was easier than I thought.

I called Tony later that evening and told him the news.

"Congratulations! That's awesome! I'm glad you decided to work for free!"

Tony's excitement radiated at me through the telephone. I could hear he was genuinely excited and was happy that I had opened a new door to opportunity.

Over the next 24 months I worked on and off for the speaker. When he came to town, I would dress up in a black, boxy, double-breasted suit that my mother had bought me to play wedding gigs. I would greet people at the door like a church greeter, as they would file into the speaker's events. I would show up early at 6 a.m. and help the speaker's team put the room together. I would stay late and help stack up the chairs and I got to observe the operation from the inside out.

Tony was an employee of the speaker's company and his job was to sell and raise money for the private real-estate deals that the speaker's company was offering.

They called these deals "Private Equity," which is essentially a fancy term for real estate or business opportunities that are not readily offered to the public like stocks, bonds, or mutual funds.

The speaker had a simple business model: educate the audience for 3 hours, teach them enough to create a desire to invest, and then encourage them to book a coffee appointment with Tony. Very clean, very simple.

Tony was a nice guy, but a bad salesman—in fact he was awful. He was far too analytical and had a slow and patronizing voice. Poor Tony couldn't close his way out of paper bag, but he still made a ton of sales because the customers were so scared of losing more money in the market and saw real estate as an asset that could never lose. The business model was so easy, so transparent, so open, and so free—I loved everything about it. This speaker was selling his deals from stage in a non-salesman-like way, he was educating instead of selling—and the customers loved it! By the time Tony sat down with them for coffee, they were sold and Tony just had to fill out the paperwork. To me, raising money for real estate looked like shooting fish in a barrel and I wanted to be the one holding the gun.

SELF MADE LESSONS:

1. Opportunity is always hiding in plain sight.

2. Working for free is one of the best ways to learn about a business.

3. Private real estate and business opportunities are hard to find, but typically offer better returns than publicly offered investments.

Visit <u>SelfMadeConfessions.com</u> for more lessons.

Confession #12

DON'T QUIT YOUR DAY JOB

"Nothing in this world can take the place of persistence. Talent will not: nothing is more common than unsuccessful men with talent. Genius will not; unrewarded genius is almost a proverb. Education will not: the world is full of educated derelicts. Persistence and determination alone are omnipotent."

CALVIN COOLIDGE

There is nothing more dangerous than a half-educated man, and although I felt like I was fully educated by virtue of spending thousands of dollars on education, I was more ignorant than ever. In martial arts, novice fighters are marked with a white circle to indicate their purity of mind. These novice fighters are safe because they act on their instincts and can dodge a blow or naturally throw a crude, but effective, punch. When the novices graduate to an intermediate, they are marked with a half-black, half-white circle and this is the most dangerous part of the training.

At the intermediate level, the fighter is no longer a novice and he second-guesses his natural moves. He is conflicted in his mind as it tries to recall the lessons from his training during combat. If an intermediate gets in a fight, either his opponent will hurt him or his ignorance, or both.

At the mastery level, the master is marked with a pure white circle, like a novice, because his mind is pure. The master has internalized his training and he fights with the natural flow of battle. If you are in a fight, the most dangerous person to be, as a fighter, is an intermediate. In the fight of real estate, I was the intermediate.

After working for free and taking some courses, I felt as though I knew enough to go into business for myself, when in fact, I was in great danger of wiping myself out financially.

Between my real-estate studies and working for free, I had become more and more disillusioned with my $10/hour call center job. I felt over-worked and underappreciated and although the company did everything they could to create a nice atmosphere with catering on Fridays and a professional dress code that made everyone feel valuable, nothing they could do would keep me.

In hindsight, I was greedy, whiney, and entitled. I needed a cold hard dose of reality. I felt that I was worth much more than they were paying me and although I was a skilled phone salesman and was consistently one of the highest selling salesmen in the office, I felt that after a few months of working there, I should have had an ownership stake in the company. I was a bad employee who should have never been hired and in truth, I am fundamentally unemployable. I'm too much of a free spirit, don't follow orders, and ruthlessly challenge authority.

It wasn't long before I began to butt heads with human resources and the company in general. I wanted to do things my way, and at the time, I thought I was being smart, entrepreneurial, and helping the company. In hindsight as a business owner today, I was being unruly, rude, and stupid. If I had an employee like myself at 22, I would have fired myself on the spot.

Businesses are complex to build and the value of the business is the peo-ple and systems that are assembled in a profitable way. There is no value in the labor itself, but rather the team that has been built and the systems. Equity in business, or ownership in the business, is calculated by measur-ing the value that the entrepreneur brings to the table, minus his labor. I had the folly and pious attitude that my labor was worth more than ev-eryone else's and consequently, I quit my job to become an entrepreneur full-time. I thought I could do it better than they could.

I remember coming home on the bus after quitting my call center job and sitting down at my mother's kitchen table. This was supposed to be an exciting moment about my freedom, but I was stunned, scared, and full of fear when faced with reality. I had $10,000 of credit card debt and

I still had some regular guitar students who could help me service the monthly payments. It was foolish of me to cut off my $10/hour full time job at this time. Effectively, I had just stepped into quicksand and I was slowly sinking. If I didn't make a move, and a good move quickly, I would sink to the bottom.

At the time my emotions told me that quitting was the right thing to do. I felt deep down in my heart that quitting was right, but now I realized that my decisions based on feelings are not always the best decisions. Freedom isn't free and I had not paid the price for my freedom. I thought I had paid the tuition to the school of life and felt entitled to be an entrepreneur.

But I was dead wrong.

Now that I was unemployed, I decided that I would wake up every day and play "real-estate businessman" much like little girls play "house." The little girls have a cardboard box that they call a house; they have a little doll they call a baby; one little girl pretends to be the mom, and the other pretends to be the dad. The little girls playing is very cute to watch, but they make no mistake; they are only playing.

There is no real house.

The little girls are not running an actual house with actual bills, utilities, mortgage payments, kids, cars, loans, and a real spouse. The little girls are playing make-believe—it's a game. The first time I quit my job and decided to play "businessman," it was very much a game or even a simulation. Instead of jumping into the pool, I really only had one foot in because I was still earning income from my part-time guitar-teaching job.

To further cushion myself from reality, I lived in the safety of my mother's home and a meager price for a room. In reality, I had no employees and no real business skills: just a head full of abstract theory, and I would sit around all day and pretend to be productive. I printed business cards, started a corporation, wrote a business plan, called Realtors and wasted their time, and looked at deals on paper, but didn't really accomplish any work. Looking back on this experience, I realize that I had become my father. I was really just a salesman who decided that he wanted to play "businessman."

It was fake. I was a fake. I looked busy, but I did nothing, produced nothing, and was nothing. The game was all about appearance and ego; it had nothing to do with creating greater value in the world or solving problems.

I had stepped into the jungle as a pious, ignorant kid who produced nothing and the jungle was very honest with me. Pious, ignorant kids don't last long in the jungle of business. The jungle tears them apart and sends them back to their mother in pieces and I learned first hand. Within a week I realized that I still had no cash—and no credit. Little had changed since my early days.

I was busy, but not productive, and very quickly, my fantasy and make-believe was over. I had to go crawling back into the shelter of another job to shield myself from the harsh environment of the real world. I knew what it looked like to be in business; I knew what the appearance was. I emulated what a businessman looked like, but still had a lot of growing and learning before I would become real.

SELF MADE LESSONS

1. A half-educated mind is a dangerous mind.

2. Hire for aptitude; fire for attitude.

3. Labor does not entitle a worker to equity in a company; equity is the value brought minus labor.

4. Always have a second income… just in case.

5. Real business is about solving problems, not appearances or ego.

6. Busy does not equal productive!

Visit SelfMadeConfessions.com for more lessons.

Confession #13

PERSISTENCE WINS, YOU FAIL ONLY WHEN YOU QUIT

"Success consists of going from failure to failure
without loss of enthusiasm."

WINSTON CHURCHILL

I was jobless and I was hopeless. I had tried to play "businessman" and had failed miserably. I had looked the part and was busy, but didn't actually transact any business. Feeling deflated, I began to take up my summertime student activity of leafing through newspapers looking for jobs to support my lifestyle.

Every summer when university was finished, I always had to get a job to pay for the upcoming tuition and books. I hated the process of finding a job because the jobs offered in the paper were always low-pay, meaningless exercises that had nothing to do with my dream of being a rock star. Every summer, summer after summer, I painted schools, houses, or other buildings for $10/hour. It didn't make sense to quit my $10/hour call center job and go back to work as a painter for $10/hour.

The newspaper was full of low-end, entry-level, dead-end jobs and the more qualified jobs required specific education, which I didn't have. I closed the newspaper and dragged my defeated body upstairs to search online for the security and shelter that a new job would provide.

I turned on my computer and did what most unproductive people do: I began to check my e-mails. Perhaps there was hope of finding a job in my inbox. By chance, there was an e-mail from the company that Tony worked for. It read that the position he had in Winnipeg was now available and they were taking applications.

The title read "Investment Advisor," which satisfied my ego and the pay was a salary plus commission, which made me feel safe. The ad promised an opportunity to earn over $100,000 per year, which really appealed to my ambition. I had finally found the perfect opportunity and for the first time in my life, I had found a job that I actually wanted to do. Real estate had become my new rock'n'roll, and this investment job, unlike any other job I had ever had, would help me to work to learn, not to earn. I immediately dusted off my résumé and sent it off to the company. Hope had been restored to my life because I saw this job as a path to learn many of the skills I was missing—mainly direct selling. The difference between a "wantrepreneur," someone who wishes to be an entrepreneur, and a real "entrepreneur" is usually the ability to sell. When I played pretend businessman, the reason why I failed to transact business was that I didn't know how to sell.

I couldn't organize my day in a productive way and I didn't know how to find leads or prospects. To sum up my short career as an entrepreneur, I had jumped into the pool with both feet and had drowned. This position as an investment advisor would help me learn the essential skill of raising money, one of my biggest obstacles to running a real-estate business. Furthermore, I would also learn how a real business worked.

I was ecstatic; nothing was more exciting than pursing my dream every minute of every day. In music, I had always pursued my dream part-time and struggled to make a living. For the first time ever, I had the opportunity to pursue my real-estate passion full-time and be unapologetic about it.

Each day that passed after sending in my résumé was a crescendo of excitement. Each day I eagerly checked the mail waiting for a letter from the company. One fateful day, I opened my mother's mailbox and inside was a letter from the company; the envelope was branded with their logo and printed in full color. I could visualize myself working in my new position, raising money, wearing a suit, speaking onstage, feeling powerful, and being a success each day. I brought the envelope into the house and sat down at the kitchen table to open it.

Inside this envelope was the answer to all of my problems. If I landed the job, then my life would change forever and I would never be stuck as a "wantrepreneur" ever again. I unfolded the letter and it read, "We are sorry, but we did not select you for this position."

My heart sank and I felt a deep despair. In front of me, I saw my path shining brightly. Yet, the letter held in my hands instantly blocked the path. I folded up the letter and put it in a drawer as if hiding it would hide the pain of rejection.

Weeks passed and a second e-mail came calling for an "investment advisor." I sent off another résumé and this time I got an interview. I met with a mountain of man named Lloyd, who flew in from Alberta to meet me. We met in a hotel restaurant; he sat on one side of the table in a gray suit, with tanned skin and slick black hair.

I sat on the other side of the table in the boxy, double-breasted black suit that my mother bought me for Christmas. I was nervous, and felt my ribs shake as I sat in the restaurant booth. This man held my whole world in his hands. I brought a copy of the business plan I had made for my fantasy real-estate company along with other small business projects I had done. I even printed out a personality test that said I was perfect for sales. I wanted to impress him, so I went above and beyond. Lloyd and I talked for an hour and a half and I felt that the interview was going well. He thanked me for coming in and a few weeks later when I got home, I got another branded letter from the company.

Expecting success, I happily opened the envelope like a birthday card from Grandma. I expected to feel the joy and love that a birthday card would bring. I imagined the birthday excitement of opening an envelope filled with a freshly pressed $20 bill that Grandma generously gave every year. The rush of excitement climaxed as I pulled the enclosed letter out of the envelope and slowly the white paper inside. It read, "We are sorry, but we did not select you for this position."

I felt a numb pain in my face and covered my eyes to hide my shame. I couldn't figure out what I had done wrong. I had prepared carefully for the interview, I had extra materials, I said the right things, I dressed up in my best suit, and I smiled as big as I could. I had a 1.5-hour interview with Lloyd and we seemed to be getting along fine, but I was still rejected.

I felt the opportunity of a lifetime slip through my fingers for a second time and I was back to square one: no job, no money, no credit, no skills, and no future. The colors of the world turned paler in that moment as my vision faded from vivid color to a dull gray tone.

Some weeks later another e-mail came from the company, announcing that the same position I had applied for had still not been filled. This time I sent in another résumé, landed another interview, and this time it was with the head of human resources; her name was Michelle. This time we met at the newly opened Winnipeg office that was freshly painted, with new furniture, but devoid of people. The space was begging for employees to bring it to life. I sat across from the boardroom table and looked at her in the eyes and said, "I have volunteered on and off for this company for quite some time; I've applied twice and I'm going to keep applying until you hire me."

She looked at me and smiled. "OK, we would like to offer you the position."

The struggle was over.

In the words of Gandhi, "First they ignore you, then they laugh at you, then they fight you, then you win." I had made one of the most important sales of my life. I was not brilliant, I was not different, I had no special voodoo techniques or Jedi mind tricks, just sheer persistence and brute force. I wasn't sure if the company had always been so difficult to land a job at, but I could see that they recruited only winners. The fact that I had applied three times after volunteering was impressive; it was like joining the US Navy Seals—many apply, but few succeed. I felt elite, like I had just been accepted into the best sales force in the world.

SELF MADE CONFESSIONS

1. The best job opportunities are not advertised in the paper.

2. The ability to sell is the most important skill of an entrepreneur.

3. Persistence wins; you fail only when you quit.

Visit <u>SelfMadeConfessions.com</u> for more lessons.

Confession #14

IF YOU CAN SELL A VACUUM, YOU CAN SELL ANYTHING!

"Sales are contingent upon the attitude of the salesman—
not the attitude of the prospect."

W. CLEMENT STONE

Within two weeks the company flew me out to Edmonton. I packed all my best clothes and hopped on the plane to head west. I didn't need to pack much because my burning ambition and persistence seemed to push me through every obstacle so far.

Flying across the country on a ticket that I had earned by selling myself into my dream job made me feel invincible. Arriving at the head office was a stunning experience: everything was new, polished, glass, and shiny. The girls working the desk were gorgeous, young, attractive, and poised models that men of any age or background would kill to possess. The men in the office were striking as well. They were tall, handsome, and extroverted and dressed to kill. They wore sharp tailored suits, shiny, black-polished oxford shoes, and crisp starched white shirts. The entire office dripped of sex, which the company bottled and sold as investment advice. The company had a winning formula: hire young hot female models to work in the office, who would attract young aggressive alpha males to work as salesmen. These men were supermen: tall and bright. They were also ideal for the financial industry—smart, hungry, and poor. The culture was vibrant, visceral, and they accepted only the best.

I felt as though I had joined a winning team and it was a team that I wanted to be part of. The salesmen were polished, both in the way they spoke and the way they looked. If they were diamonds, I was only rough lump of coal. I couldn't compete with their image or sharp wit and vocabulary.

They sat me down in the boardroom with another young recruit named David, who was later nicknamed Buck by some of the alpha males in the office. Buck was also a rough lump of coal with a shaggy haircut that had grown wild around his ears and badly needed trimming. However, underneath his shaggy hair, Buck fit the description: tall, handsome, athletic, and smart. With the right polish, Buck would make a great salesman. We sat in the boardroom and four men entered the room. Two were executives from the company, barely a few years older than me. These executives were different from the visceral alpha male salesmen. They were more effeminate, polished, and nerdy with glasses. The other two men were much older, either in their fifties or sixties.

I quickly learned that the two nerdy men were here to train me and Buck. They were unbelievably young, but they were executives, so we treated them like experts. We sat in the boardroom for a full day, learning how to organize and take notes.

To my surprise, that one full day was the entire extent of the training program for the company and although I was in Edmonton for 7 days of training, they had no further content to teach me about sales. The two older men who sat with Buck and me were newly hired by the company as sales consultants and were assigned to us as mentors.

There was very little briefing or introduction to our new mentors, but I quickly learned that these two older men had spent their entire life selling vacuum cleaners door to door. These men were proven warriors in the art of direct sales. They had sharpened and perfected their tools, selling every day for their entire adult lives. The moment I learned that my mentors were professional vacuum cleaner salesmen, I began to cringe.

The nagging voice of my mother entered my brain and I felt as though I was in the wrong place. My palms started to sweat and my fingers formed into fists as I felt the urge to stand up and run out the door. I thought I was selling investments, not vacuum cleaners! What did these men know about selling investments? I suddenly felt dirty, but at the same time my life had finally come full circle.

When I was seventeen, I was looking for a summer job and the only way I knew how was the newspaper. I scoured the classifieds and noticed an ad that read, "Make $85 per hour!" My heart jumped the minute I saw that kind of pay and I immediately dialed the number in the ad. A young pretty voice answered the other end of the telephone and she told me to come to the office tomorrow at 10 a.m. and "dress sharp."

After I hung up the phone, I immediately dialed my grandmother to tell her the great news that I had a job interview and that I wanted to borrow her car to drive across town to get the job. I arrived in an industrial part of town full of derelict homes, train tracks, and empty warehouses. I quickly located the building where my interview was to be held and parked on a side street. The building was a blank brick industrial bunker with no windows and only one mirrored-glass door on the front; no sign, no markings, completely anonymous. I knocked on the door at 10 a.m. for my appointment and no one answered, so I went back to Grandma's car and waited for 10 minutes. I went back to the front door at 10:10 a.m. and the door pushed open, revealing a beautiful reception area. A young handsome man in his late twenties introduced himself to me as "Mr. Ellice." He had a huge white smile from ear to ear and was dressed in a perfectly tailored and pressed dark navy suit. I felt uneasy about the unmarked building and the fact that no one was there to answer the door at 10 a.m., but Mr. Ellice's appearance and demeanor made me feel at ease.

I sat in the lobby and filled out the application forms for the $85-per-hour job and surprisingly, there was no one else in the lobby applying for this position. Maybe I was in luck. Finally, Mr. Ellice called me into his office around the corner and I handed him the forms I had filled out. He looked at my résumé and the forms I had spent 15 minutes filling out and then quickly pushed the papers aside. Instead, we talked about my dreams of being a rock star. After about 15 minutes of banter Mr. Ellice said, "I've got three positions available in my company: one is for secretaries, but you don't want that… another is my warehouse guys, but you're smarter than that… and the third are my sales guys. I overpay everyone and I think you would be best suited to sales because you're a great guy to talk to! I want you to call me today at 5:00 p.m. and I'll let you know if you got the job."

I felt very excited to have made it this far in the interview process and quickly asked Mr. Ellice what I was going to be selling. He replied, "It's a cleaning product about the size of a football and it's going to change the world!"

"Wow," I thought to myself… *I'm going to change the world!*

I drove back to my grandmother's house and as I returned the keys for her car, I told her I was going to be selling something: "a cleaning product the size of a football that would change the world!" My 84-year-old grandmother lit up with excitement and as a lady who grew up on a farm, she was always excited when anyone in her family got a new job. My grandmother was also very curious about my pitch and the cleaning products that would change the world. She was so curious and promised to buy whatever I was selling. I was so excited; I already had a sale before I even knew what I would be selling!

I called back Mr. Ellice at 5:00 p.m. on the nose. He answered the phone and said, "Stefan, I'm so glad you called; out of the 80 interviews I did today, you were the only guy I wanted to talk to. Come in tomorrow for training and orientation. It's a three-day, unpaid training, but on Monday morning we'll have you making money right away!"

Then he hung up the phone. I felt as though I had won the lottery: $85 per hour was a lot of money, more than 10 times the minimum wage at the time. I didn't think about the fact that it would be impossible to do 80 interviews in one day. I didn't think that I would be the only one calling him back at 5:00 pm, but I didn't care; I felt like I had won the lottery.

The next morning I showed up at the unmarked bunker and was ushered into a back room. Inside the room were five young sales candidates sitting in chairs wanting the same job I did. They were young, good looking, and dressed to kill. Out of the five sales candidates, one was a former Xerox salesman, one was an ex-car salesman, one was a med student, one was a single mother, and the other was a student like me. Mr. Ellice greeted us at 9 a.m. and we all waited eagerly to see the product we would be selling, but first, we were introduced to Clancy.

Clancy was the owner of the company, in his midforties, with skin that was so tanned that he looked like a baseball glove. He had a pencil-thin moustache and was balding with a bad black greasy comb-over. He wore a yellow dress shirt that was unbuttoned far too low and he had a beer belly that hung over his belt. I wasn't sure if his beer belly was from drinking beer or just working too hard and living the salesman life. He had multiple gold chains around his neck and far too many gold rings on his fingers. He looked like a wrestling promoter, a low-level pimp, or a Mafioso. His intense black eyes fixated on us from behind his horn-rimmed glasses and he took the stage from Mr. Ellice quietly and intensely.

"Are you guys ready to see what you're going to be selling?" Clancy asked.

"YES!" We cried out in unison; we were all high on the idea of making fast, easy money.

"Alright, let me show you." Clancy pointed to a box behind him that was covered with a black sheet the size of a large microwave. Like a magician, he grabbed one end of the black curtain and whipped the curtain like he was pulling a rabbit out of a hat. The excitement peaked and suddenly, we were all staring at a generic brown cardboard box.

The room was silent. We were all looking at this box, but no one could identify what was inside. Mr. Ellice, Clancy's magic show assistant, got down on his knees and opened the box quickly, as if the magic was wearing off the presentation. Finally, he pulled out a shiny, metallic, space age-looking machine...

Mr. Ellice held up the machine like a prized fish that he had caught in a fishing championship. We all stared at it, mystified at its beauty, but unable to identify what we were looking at until finally someone said:

"It's a vacuum!"

"A vacuum?" I thought to myself. "I can't sell vacuums! Vacuum cleaner salesmen are slimy and I'm not slimy!"

My internal dialog was outraged. I had driven across town twice, sat through meetings, and now I was being sold on selling vacuums. I knew that everyone in the room wanted to leave the minute we realized that Clancy and Mr. Ellice had tricked us into watching their vacuum presentation, but we were too polite and we were already committed, so no one dared to leave.

Mr. Ellice dazzled us with the unbelievable features and benefits of this space-age vacuum. It was a truly impressive machine, built with a mini jet engine inside, and it would last for 40 years. He told us the backstory of the machine and the fact that it was built in a retooled jet engine factory from World War II. He told us about the magnesium finish that was nearly indestructible, and it would bounce but not dent if you threw the vacuum across a cement driveway (which Mr. Ellice informed us was one extreme way to close a sale). The hose of the machine was made of neoprene, the same material that they make deep sea diving wet suits out of and finally, Mr. Ellice dumped 15 pounds of sand into the vacuum, opened the door, and dumped the sand on his head, but magically, the sand did not fall out. The amazing jet engine flow of air was flowing so strong through the machine that it held the 15 pounds of sand magically in place when a lesser machine would have the sand dump onto Mr. Ellice's head. When I saw the sand trick, I was sold—I wanted to be a vacuum salesman!

After nearly an hour of watching the magic show, we were all sold on selling vacuums and Clancy took the stage as things began to get serious: "How much money do you want for selling one of these things?" Clancy's tone was confrontational and he stared us down like a thug while he slowly walked over to a sales flip chart.

No one said anything. We were too intimidated.

"Six hundred dollars?" Clancy barked.

There was no response. The room was silent.

"Six hundred bucks for selling one of these things?" Clancy asked rhetorically as he continued to stare us down. He wrote a big $600 on the flip chart without breaking eye contact with us, and still no one moved.

We had no idea about what was a fair commission to sell a vacuum, but $600 did sound appealing to me. If I only sold one vacuum a week, I would be making way more money than my other summer jobs painting houses.

"How about seven hundred dollars?" Clancy wrote $700 in huge numbers on the flip chart and we began to squirm.

Seven hundred sounded even better.

"How about eight hundred dollars?" Clancy wrote a huge $800 on the flip chart and we began to look at each other and smile. I couldn't believe it. Selling vacuums suddenly seemed to be the best thing since sliced bread.

"Listen, you guys sell one in a week, I'll pay you six hundred dollars a sale. You sell two in a week, I'll pay you seven hundred dollars per sale, and if you sell three in a week, I'll pay you eight hundred dollars a sale!" Clancy began to circle the $800 on the flip chart and I began to grin, thinking I was going to make more money than I ever had in my life by selling vacuums. Suddenly, my enthusiasm for this machine began to swell and my beliefs about selling vacuums began to instantly change.

I spent the next three days in training and every half day, one of the sales candidates would drop out. We would come back from lunch and there would be one less person in the room. After three days, I was the only one left.

"It's time to do some real live demos," Clancy said at the end of the third day. "If you do six demos, whether you sell or not, I'll give you a hundred and fifty bucks... It's not much, but it will help you buy some bread and sandwich meat on Monday morning."

I pictured myself buying a few loafs on rye bread and deli ham to survive the week. Getting into sales was becoming real for me. I could even imagine tasting the ham, rye bread, and yellow hot dog mustard that I had earned by selling.

I had worked for three days for no pay and was beginning to get hungry from not earning any money. The idea of $150 appealed to me greatly and I knew that it wouldn't be that difficult to show this vacuum to my friends and family. The idea of buying some bread and meat also seemed appealing. I wanted to earn my sustenance for the week instead of living on handouts from Mom.

I took one of the vacuums home and called everyone I knew to make my six presentations. My mother fought me every day when I came home from sales training: "Sales is a hard life! Your father always wanted to sell, but he didn't make any money! Sales companies always screw you out of commissions!" All along the way my mother relentlessly barraged me with negativity until the third day, when I emotionally collapsed.

For those three days I had attended sales training eight hours each day, came home, and fought with my mother for eight hours and then slept for eight hours. Life became a grind.

Finally, on Monday I showed up at the office and gave my demo vacuum back with tears in my eyes. I was frustrated and wanted to see if I could make it in sales. "Mr. Ellice, I quit. My mother doesn't support me doing this and every day when I go home, she fights with me. I'm exhausted and I just can't do this..."

Mr. Ellice looked at me in the eyes and said, "That's fine. Maybe this isn't for you. Just let me ask you one question. Will your mother stop you from doing other things you want to do in your life?"

"No, I don't think so." I said, meekly staring at the floor. I told Mr. Ellice with my words that my mother would never hold me back, but in my heart, I wasn't sure. I returned the vacuum in the same cardboard box I had borrowed it in and left the sales office forever.

Years later when I was assigned my mentor in the sales office in Alberta, I knew I was in the right place in my life. I had wanted to sell vacuums years ago and now I was right where I belonged, back with the vacuum sales-men, earning my bread and ham. Some people believe in fate. I believe there are certain people in life you are destined to meet, and sometimes you just don't meet them right away. Somehow, through fate, everyone ends up where they belong. My heart had wanted to sell vacuums years ago and now my current mentors were vacuum salesmen. Steve Jobs says, "You can only connect the dots looking backwards," and now I could see there was a bigger reason why my vacuum dreams were put on hold. In the big picture, my place was to sell real-estate investments instead of vacuums. I just couldn't see the big picture when I was younger.

SELF MADE LESSONS

1. Perception is reality and sex sells.

2. Vacuum salesmen are some of the most skilled salesmen in the world. If you want to learn to sell, try selling something that no one wants to buy!

3. If you can sell vacuums, you can sell anything (including investments).

4. The harder the item is to sell, the higher your skills as a salesman need to be. The harder the item is to sell, the higher your income will be!

Visit <u>SelfMadeConfessions.com</u> for more lessons.

Confession #15

NO ONE WANTS TO DATE
A BROKE GUY

"Style is a reflection of your attitude and your personality."

Shawn Ashmore

Day 2 of training was about to start and Buck and I were sitting in the boardroom, like two lumps of coal waiting to be pressurized into diamonds. We sat and waited, and waited, and waited, until finally one of the nerd executives walked. He informed us that the management didn't have anything planned for the day. So instead of classroom training, I was going to be sent into the field with Luke, one of the company's top salesmen.

Buck was going into the field with someone else. As Buck left the room, I started to get nervous and think that it was too early to start selling. The little voice in my head whined that I didn't know enough theory and wasn't confident about my product. Self-doubt is a bummer.

Suddenly, Luke walked into the boardroom. "Aarnio, get in the car, we're going to Lloyd (which was short for Lloydminster)."

Luke was six foot four; blond and built like the Terminator. He used to play in the Western Hockey League, which farm team for the NHL, but he dislocated his shoulder three times. With too many injuries, Luke had to quit hockey. He was a goon, a hit man, and the fighter on the team that would go out onto the ice and beat people up.

day, if you typed Luke's name into Google, you would find videos of unching other hockey players in the face and beating down weaker opponents on the ice. He was the kind of guy you wanted to fight the war with, but you never wanted to fight against. Luke's posture was perfect: he stood tall, arched his back, and had his shoulders all the way back, which made his chest look huge. In his perfectly tailored suit and white shirt, he was intimidating, but trustworthy. He strode confidently in his perfectly polished black oxford shoes with a thin elegant point. His handshake was firm, but not overpowering, which inspired trust.

Luke was a diamond and I was a lump of coal by contrast. My baggy unfitted dress clothes made me look like a clown next to him. I did my best, but I couldn't compete with his posture, his stance, or his outfit. In contrast to Luke's appearance, I had black pleated parachute pants that didn't fit me property, a white pirate shirt that was too big and didn't fit my body, a gray vest I had purchased at a thrift store, and a $1 burgundy tie I had bought with the vest. At the very best, I looked like hotel staff; at the worst, I looked like a very tame pirate. I didn't know it at the time, but my image was seriously hurting my ability to sell and was costing me thousands of dollars in lost opportunity every year.

Earlier that summer I had asked one girl out on a date ten times and in the same summer I was rejected ten times. I had a mentor named Howard and Howard was in his sixties. He was a professional disc jockey, a local radio legend, and a big fan of my rock band while it was still alive. Howard had unbelievable taste in music, fashion, and women, and the fact that he took a liking to my music was a huge compliment.

After my band broke up, Howard called me and invited me to play at a little Italian bistro that played live music every Tuesday. I was flattered that Howard invited me, so I showed up early, brought my guitar, and got ready to play a few songs by myself. No band, just me and my guitar. Before going onstage, Howard pulled me aside and whispered in his low booming radio voice, "There's someone I want you to meet."

Howard took me to the other side of the restaurant and said, "Stefan, meet Céline."

As I heard his words, I looked up in front of me and standing before me was a stunning beauty. She had long blonde mermaid hair, huge blue eyes, and a voluptuous figure. She was eighteen, a student, and made extra money waitressing tables at the local Italian bistro.

Howard introduced her to me as a girl who wrote a fashion column in the free press, and he sold me as a cool musician. On the surface, she was way out of my league. I had long scruffy musician hair, a Led Zeppelin T-shirt, and brown denim pants that didn't fit. She was dressed in a black dress that clung to her perfect body that was accented with her flowing blonde hair. Time froze as I shook her hand, and then it sped up as I was rushed onstage. I played my set, but she left before I could talk to her.

I would show up at the Italian bistro every Tuesday to hang out with Howard. Howard was pure charisma. He looked amazing, he sounded amazing, and he knew how to connect people and make them feel amazing. I decided that I would see Howard religiously every Tuesday and silently absorb his lessons.

Whatever Howard wanted to talk about, we talked about. Whatever Howard ate, we ate. Whomever Howard wanted to meet, we met. It was an interesting experience being a fly on the wall in Howard's world for one night a week. He was riveting, persuasive, and influential. I got to watch the master at work.

"Céline's been asking about you," Howard would whisper in my ear in his low booming radio voice. "You should ask her out!'

In hindsight, I wasn't sure if Céline was actually asking about me, or if Howard was just living vicariously through me because he was sixty years old. At his age, it was inappropriate for him to hit on eighteen-year-old girls. Either way, Howard breathed enough courage into my ear to make me confident enough to ask Céline out on a date.

Céline would be busy waiting tables and I would catch her on a break or between tables, strike up some canned conversation, and propose that we go play Frisbee in the park on the weekend. She would look at me with a sideways glance and say, "Maybe, baby."

The two words that I hate the most in the English language are "maybe, baby." For the next 10 weeks I would do the same routine over and over again. I would go see Howard, play a little music, chase Céline around, and hear her say: "Maybe, baby."

Finally one Tuesday, Howard said, "I've got some men's magazines for you... Come out to my car and I'll give them to you."

"Men's magazines?" I thought to myself. "What am I going to do with men's magazines?"

"There's great articles in them, great information, come out to the car!" beckoned Howard in his persuasive deep tone. I followed Howard out to the parking lot across the street and he opened the trunk of his car, revealing a huge stack of *GQ* magazines. *GQ* stands for "Gentlemen's Quarterly" and it's filled with contemporary men's fashion and facets of the modern gentlemen's lifestyle. At the time I had never seen *GQ* before and couldn't see any value in reading the publication. Howard picked up the massive stack of magazines that seemed to weigh at least 50 pounds and loaded them into my hands. I took the stack of magazines home and put them on my dresser, not knowing what to do with them. They were covered in pictures of men in suits wearing clothes that I couldn't afford, so I didn't see how they would be relevant to my life.

The next Tuesday I would arrive at the bistro and Howard would ask, "Did you read the articles in the *GQs* I gave you?" Howard would look at me straight in the eyes and exclaim, "Great articles in those magazines!"

"Yeah, Howard... I did." In truth, I was lying through my teeth. I had stacked up the magazines on my dresser but had not found the willpower or the interest to open them yet.

"I'm glad you like them!" Howard replied, "Come to the car, I have more for you!"

"More?" I silently screamed on the inside.

So I followed Howard back to his car in the same parking lot across the street and he opened his trunk, revealing another stack of *GQs*. I couldn't figure out where Howard got all these magazines from, but he was such an avid fashion aficionado that he had subscriptions to British *GQ*, American *GQ*, Canadian *GQ*, as well as *Esquire* and *Details*. I took the second stack of magazines and began to lament my situation. Why was Howard giving me all of these magazines? These magazines had nothing to do with me and I wanted nothing to do with them!

I took the magazines home and stacked them on top of the others. The pile was almost five feet high and my shelf began to buckle under the weight. I called my friends, trying to give the magazines away for free, but no one wanted them. I didn't have the heart to throw them out, so I started an attempt to read the articles: I read one article, "The Life of a Soldier in the War in Afghanistan," followed by "How to Pick Up a Prostitute in Las Vegas." The articles didn't seem to relate to my life, but I committed to reading them so I could impress Howard.

The next Tuesday I went back to the Italian bistro and told Howard about the articles I had read. He looked at me blankly and said, "I'm glad you're reading them." That was the end of the discussion about the GQs.

After being hired by the company and flying out to Edmonton for training, Luke and I loaded Luke's Jeep with sales materials and began the drive to Lloydminster to conduct Luke's sales presentations. I was anxious to watch Luke sell because I heard he was one of the top salesmen in the company and I was excited to see him in action.

When we arrived at the hotel in Lloydminster, we prepared the boardroom where the meetings were being held and over two days conducted nearly 20 meetings. I wore my pirate costume and Luke wore his stunning tailored suit. Every meeting I watched Luke stand up to his full six-foot-four height, stretch up, almost onto his tip toes to appear even taller, and stride effortlessly across the room to meet his prospect with a powerful but gentle handshake. I watched him lean all the way back in his chair as he talked about hockey with most prospects, and I watched him flex his muscles through his shirt. As he leaned back in his chair and talked slowly and confidently with a sexual undertone, he would cross his legs in his chair, placing his heel on his knee in a way that stretched his perfectly tailored pants.

All of this sub-verbal communication was happening, but the actual selling and the actual verbiage being said at the table was disorganized. As a professional musician, I was expecting Luke to follow a routine, or a script, or a set presentation to control the outcome of the meetings. He would let his prospects walk out the door one after the other without taking an order or closing a sale and I started to get frustrated.

Finally Luke and I were alone and I felt a need to vent my frustration. "Why aren't you closing these guys?" I couldn't believe we had driven all the way to another city to not bother selling any investments.

"Aarnio, you don't close on the first meeting; just watch, I'll close these guys eventually."

I couldn't believe he didn't have a set routine and wouldn't ask for the sale on the first meeting, but he had the sales numbers to back up his method, so I let the issue go. We lay around in the boardroom during a long stretch between meetings and pulled out our smartphones. Like a couple of sad, lonely cowboys, we began to show each other Facebook pictures of every girl we "should have," "would have," and "wished we did."

First Luke would show me a few of his old hockey groupies, then I pulled out my phone, and showed him a Facebook picture of Céline sitting in a hot tub, wearing nothing but a pink bikini, holding a glass of red wine, and smiling mischievously at the camera with her enormous blue eyes and long blonde mermaid hair. "Ugh, Luke, I've asked out this girl ten times and I've got rejected ten times. What do I do?"

Luke looked at the stunning picture of Céline on my phone and then looked at me slouching in my pirate costume like a sack of potatoes. Silently, he looked back at Céline, and then locked eyes with me and said "Aarnio, if you want a girl like that, you've gotta start reading *GQ*!"

The words hit me like a ton of bricks. My heart stopped, I leaned back in my chair and thought I was going to fall forever into nothing. Howard had politely tried to tell me for weeks that I had a bad self-image, but was too polite to tell me straight. I was the punch line of my own cruel joke. It was time for change.

Luke straightened me out and took me to the hotel bathroom to show me in the mirror what was wrong with my image. My haircut was wrong; he pulled out a *GQ* magazine and showed me the right haircut for my face. He told me to throw out my pirate costume and get a properly tailored suit. He showed me everything he knew about designer cuts of fabric and having the proper fit. Looking good and having a great self-image was not just an art, but also a science.

I went home and threw out 99% of my wardrobe, which was mostly hand-me-downs from Dad, Christmas gifts from Mom, and thrift store treasures I plundered and hoarded. I immediately ordered three custom-tailored suits and when they arrived in the mail, I tore the box open and carefully slid into my brand-new navy three-piece suit. I put the ensemble together with a crisp white custom tailored shirt and a solid power tie. I had the entire image—the suit, the shirt, the hair—but I was missing the shoes, so I drove to the mall to buy a pair of black shiny oxfords to go with my new look. My entire look was complete and by chance, it was Tuesday night.

I drove to the local bistro to meet Howard in my new suit and as I walked into the building, I turned around a blind corner and locked eyes with Céline. She saw me in my new suit and I watched her eyes scan me from head to toe, then back up to my eyes. Her eyes sparkled; she smiled and said, "Wow!" in a half-breath-half-whisper.

SELF MADE LESSONS

1. People buy your image before they buy you.

2. Your image either makes you money or costs you money.

3. You need a mentor for every part of your life, including personal image.

4. Body language and tone are more important for effective communication than words spoken.

5. Getting a makeover is one of the fastest ways to increase your income!

6. Taking a risk, being open, and listening to feedback can be the best investment you ever make.

Visit SelfMadeConfessions.com for more lessons.

Confession #16

YOU HAVE TO SELL EVERY DAY!

"You don't have to be great to start,
but you have to start to be great."

ZIG ZIGLAR

After my week of training was over, the company flew me back home to Winnipeg. It was getting colder and fall was turning into winter. The head of human resources had given me the one and only key to the Winnipeg office. I was in charge of my little empire.

The Winnipeg office was located above a rental car office on a busy street in South Winnipeg. The office was invisible to the naked eye, which was bad for business. Where most people saw a rental car business or a used car parking lot, I saw the Winnipeg investment office. Unfortunately, we had no visual presence and we were located through an unmarked secret door on the wrong side of the building.

As I slid the key into the lock for the first time, I felt the excitement of being the solo operator of this office and being in charge of the entire city. I turned the key and opened the door; it was heavier than it looked and I proceeded to walk up the stairs into the dark cavernous office upstairs. I pushed open a second door and as I walked through the threshold into the main office, the future looked grim. The old gray commercial carpet was ill fitted to the floor and wrinkled up like an old man's skin. The room was completely bare of furniture and it looked like the company had gone out of business sometime ago.

A huge brown smear of mud trailed across the floor like horse manure in a dirty barn, and it looked like someone, or something, had been dragged through the manure from one end of the office to the other. A dead house-plant sat in a lonely corner of the room with a single dead limb poking out of the mud toward the heavens. To finish off the room, one lonely office desk sat in the middle of the room with a cheap executive office chair orbiting nearby. I was proud, I was excited—this office was mine!

I stood in the doorway and surveyed the room briefly; the center room was huge with many smaller offices connecting to it like a hub. All of the offices were empty and there was barely any furniture. Maybe the office had been robbed? I had heard that the office had three or four employees before they hired me, but the employees had all quit together and formed their own competing investment company. I was here to revive this dead shell and restore the office to its former glory.

I took a deep breath and then exhaled while the moisture from my breath formed a white cloud in front of me. It was winter in Winnipeg and the office had absolutely no heat. It was so cold in the office that I was surprised the pipes hadn't burst. I kept my winter jacket on as I sat down at the receptionist desk and began to set up my clunky IBM laptop.

No Internet, no printer, no fax, no scanner, no paper, no paperclips—absolutely nothing. The previous employees had raided everything from the office except for an old telephone. They left the office desk that was too heavy to carry, and a second-hand chair that had no value.

I called my sales manager from the office phone, and magically the phone line was working. I told my manager I was going to go back to my car because unlike the office, my car had heat.

My first assignment was to call 50 "third-base leads" and try to sell them an investment in a 400-unit apartment block in Arizona. The company still had to raise a couple million dollars to make the acquisition work and my manager e-mailed me a spreadsheet of 50 names and 50 telephone numbers of people who were interested, but hadn't bought. I didn't know how old the leads were, but from what I gathered, no one had contacted them in a long time.

I later learned that the salesmen in the company never ever called on "third-base leads." Instead, they would wait for the marketing road crew to blow through town and hand the salespeople a stack of hot fresh leads that were ready to buy. I wasn't really sure how the company was making money between the marketing sweeps if they didn't bother to call third-base leads. To me, any lead, even an old third-base lead, was still better than calling random names out of the phone book. So I treated my list of 50 leads like gold.

I printed the list out from my mom's home printer and sat in my car with the engine idling so I could study some of the names, phone numbers, and comments on the list. My sales manager was so new to the company that he didn't have much advice to share with me about selling. Everyone was so young and so green that the entire company seemed to sell on enthusiasm, youth, and sex—instead of sound sales practices and investment advice.

I went back to the office and paced around the empty boardroom in my winter jacket while I scribbled some notes on printer paper that I had stolen from my mother's house. My scribbles were my desperate attempt to try to make a sales presentation. The company didn't have a standard presentation and they had no flip chart or any other type of sales tool, so I had to improvise. As a musician, I expected a good sales presentation to be scripted like a sheet of music or a well-written play. To me, sales presentations should never be improvised. There is too much risk and you only have so much emotional energy to improvise each day. Once that energy is gone, you are too tired to present effectively.

Somehow I had to explain to my prospects that they were going to give my company 100% of the money to buy real estate on their behalf. Although the investors were putting up 100% of the money, they were going to receive only 33% of the ownership in the property or roughly one-third. The company I worked for took a third, and the company who supplied and managed the apartment building took another third. It was great math for the company I worked for. The company put up none of the money and took 33% of the deal.

It was also a great deal for the managing company supplying the 400-unit building because they also put up none of the money and took 33% of the deal. The investors got the short end of the stick with putting up 100% of the money, but only taking 33% of the deal, but the company advertised that the investors would earn a 15% return on their money every year, so even the investors won by getting 33% of the deal for putting up the money and doing absolutely no work.

I broke the concept down as simply as I could by drawing a triangle with three corners: the Money, the People, and the Deal.

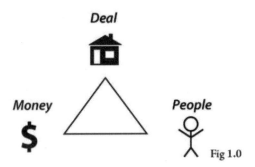

Fig 1.0

I practiced drawing the triangle and telling the story to myself over and over again about how our real-estate deals worked. Our company facilitated the Money, the People, and the Deal coming together and that was how wealth was made. The story sold me, and I would use this story to sell to my investors as a company employee and later on my own private deals.

The concept was brilliant: let someone else bring 100% of the money and give them 33% of the deal. All I had to do was supply a deal and a great team of people and I could take 66% of the deal. I watched the company do it over and over again. Later in life, when I did my own deals, I built my entire business model around bringing money, people, and deals together. I would construct the transaction and sell of equity in my deals to investors who would supply 100% of the cash.

I had cracked the code on a sustainable model for purchasing money-down real estate. This formula captured my heart and my mind. Instantly, I was in love.

SELF MADE LESSONS

1. A secret office is a bad investment; if you are going to invest in office space, make sure you have effective signage. Signs are some of the most effective marketing of all time.

2. Facts tell; stories sell. Tell the Money, People, Deal story rather than give dry facts.

3. If you don't know what you're doing, or don't have the right tools, just improvise.

4. Have faith; faith is the opposite of fear. Take action every day and make things happen!

Visit <u>MoneyPeopleDeal.com</u> to learn more about the MPD triangle!

Confession #17

THE MONEY WANTS YOU MORE THAN YOU WANT THE MONEY

"Money is only a tool. It will take you wherever you wish,
but it will not replace you as the driver."

AYN RAND

Shortly after I arrived in Winnipeg, the company sent Gerry, one of the veteran vacuum salesmen, to help me set up the office. I showed up at the airport early one morning to pick up Gerry as he flew in from the Canadian prairie town of Regina.

I was green, as green could get. Young and excited, bright eyed, and bushy tailed. My ambition was eager to get into the field and start selling. Gerry, by contrast, was tempered. He was weathered, like an old samurai that had seen a thousand battles or an original cowboy that had won the Wild West in another life. His skin was like leather, tanned, and wrinkled. But lovingly aged like a well-worn baseball glove that had been passed down from father to son.

Gerry had been through many battles in business and had served his time of nearly 30 years selling vacuums door to door all over North America. Gerry had done what I always wanted to do. He had proved himself as a salesman. He was a proven commodity in the art of selling.

Gerry was the closer who would come in at the end of the vacuum presentation and seal the deal. In the past, he managed a team of four or five salespeople who would go into homes and present a brand-new Kirby

111

vacuum. Gerry would stand outside on the street and wait for the salesmen to place the vacuum box outside the door, indicating that the presentation was over and it was time to close. Gerry would then storm the house as the "manager" and negotiate a sale on behalf of the presenting salesmen. The method was simple: the junior salesmen would tee them up, and Gerry would knock them down.

Gerry wore a long tan overcoat, travelled light for a business traveler, and although he was old, moved swiftly and had dark intelligent eyes behind his thick black-rimmed glasses. His voice was raspy like an old blues singer who had smoked a lifetime of cigarettes, but I never saw him smoke.

I drove Gerry to the Winnipeg office and as soon as he felt the cold office air and absence of heat on his face, he slowly looked around and surveyed the dead shell of an office. He instantly knew something was wrong. "Stefan, turn up the heat in here!"

"I can't. There's no way I can control that from here," I whined.

"Call the landlord. No heat? No rent! We aren't paying a lease on a building with no heat!"

Gerry was like a four-star general that had just entered a war zone. Within a few hours, he had the entire office up and running. Supplies were ordered, the Internet was running, the printer was working, and he called the landlord and threatened him to get the heat working by noon. Gerry was not only a master salesman, but he was also a seasoned businessman who had run many successful businesses over his life.

Gerry was an engineer by trade and the exact opposite of my fledgling salesman brain. Where I thought of sales as an art, as a musician thinks of a performance, Gerry thought in terms of cold, hard numbers. "Sales is a science," he said. "You have calls, conversations, appointments, and closes. You need to track and keep records of your numbers each day so you know what is working and what isn't."

"Why do I need to keep track of all that?" I asked.

"Every salesman at some point will start to deviate or improvise away from the proven system and that's where the problems happen. If you keep track of your ratios: calls to conversations, conversations to appointments, and appointments to closes, you can fix your sales machine if it breaks. Eventually, you can calculate the dollars you make every time you dial the phone."

"Why would I want to know that?"

"In sales, you need to psychologically reward yourself every time you make a call, not when you close. When you close, you are just picking up the money that you earned while dialing. Actions equal dollars, dollars don't equal actions."

I wrote the mantra "actions equal dollars" on a piece of paper on my desk and I still have it written down today.

With Gerry's help, I started to actually dial the phone and call my 50 third-base leads. Although I was at the office at 10 a.m. in the morning every day, I had to wait until about 6 p.m. to make effective calls, because most of my prospects were unavailable at work.

I dialed the phone furiously and kept meticulous notes on when I called and what the outcome of the call was. I would dial the same person every day until I finally got someone on the line. When they picked up, I would run them through my script that I read like a Hollywood actor going for an Oscar. I learned from Gerry that if I was able to get to the bottom of my script, I was going to book an appointment to sell a deal. If the prospect cut me off somewhere in the middle, then I knew that the chances of booking a meeting were almost zero.

When I dialed my first phone number, an elderly man picked up. "Hello?" His voice wavered into the receiver.

"Hi Bill, this is Stefan Aarnio from Quick Street Capital calling. How are you today?" I began my script and pushed out as much energy as I could. I wanted my energy to transfer through the phone line and capture his attention.

I continued my script and explained that no one had called from the company for a while and I felt personally responsible. I had just taken over the Winnipeg office and was just making a brief customer service call to make sure everything was OK and wanted to tell him about our new offerings that were coming up in the near future.

I asked for the meeting and Bill accepted.

Two days later, Bill showed up at the office. He was in his sixties, thin, and full of life. He carried a binder and portfolio of investments under his arm and was interested in the 15% return that I had promised him over the phone from the Arizona apartment complex the company was currently selling. Bill came in for a thirty-minute meeting, but stayed for three hours as we talked through FORM: Family, Occupation, Recreation, and Money. I then took him through my scripted presentation explaining how we put Money, People, and Deals together. Bill had been investing in mutual funds and at the time, the stock market was plummeting. Bill liked my enthusiasm and my presentation. At the end of the meeting, Bill agreed to invest $10,000.

I was shocked. Was it really that easy?

My first call and my first meeting and I had already raised $10,000.

I got up from my seat and raced to the office supply room to grab the paperwork and write up the order. I had no idea how to fill out the paperwork but fumbled through it anyways. Before the meeting was over, Bill had cut me a check and I welcomed him "to the family."

After sending Bill out of the office, I was ecstatic to show Gerry the first check I had produced. I had raised my first $10,000 of real estate and did not even have my license to sell investments yet. The office in Edmonton couldn't believe that I had sold a "third-base lead." To them, those leads were dead. To me, the leads were a goldmine of untapped potential.

The entire money-raising process, although it seemed long and complicated to learn, was quite simple in reality. In the end, I learned a lesson I would never forget: the money always wants you more than you want the money.

SELF MADE LESSONS

1. Consider a mentor who has an opposite style to you. Opposite styles will force you to think differently and grow faster.

2. Sales is both an art and a science.

3. Actions equal dollars; dollars don't equal actions.

4. When selling on the phone, always use a script. Scripts will save your energy and give you more control over the outcome of the call.

5. There are thousands of dollars of untapped potential in "old" leads and dormant databases. Leads cost money to acquire! Databases cost companies thousands or even millions of dollars to build. They are one of the most valuable assets in the company and must be utilized by the sales force every day to maximize revenue.

Visit <u>SelfMadeConfessions.com</u> for more lessons.

Confession #18

YOU WILL BE ABANDONED
AT SOME POINT

"No one's ever achieved financial fitness with a January
resolution that's abandoned by February."

SUZE ORMAN

In my days of volunteering at the company, I was like a church usher wearing my oversized, boxy, black double-breasted suit. I greeted people at the door, showed them to their seats, and stood at the back of the room while listening to the sermon. Anything that was required of me, I did. I liked volunteering because it gave me an inside view into the world of investment real estate. I got to study and observe a real living company that raised millions of dollars to make large real-estate investments. Another perk of volunteering was the people I met.

While standing at the back of the room at one event, I met a young bright Realtor in his earlier twenties named John Mark. He was young, tall, dark, and handsome with kind brown eyes. We started chatting and he told me that he was buying his first triplex with his business partner. I had not bought any investment real estate yet, but at the time, I was saving up and had a full-time salaried job. My salary qualified me for mortgages and I was looking for a property myself. We shook hands, exchanged business cards, and promised to stay in touch.

A few days later, John Mark called me and invited me to play "Cash Flow," a board game like monopoly that taught the players how to invest in business, real estate, and stocks. I was excited to meet other young hungry real-estate enthusiasts and graciously accepted.

A few days later on a Wednesday night, I parked my car outside of a large apartment building on Queen Street and buzzed the intercom to come in. I met John Mark and his partner in a small concrete condo where I and five other strangers huddled around a single board game. It was like we were having a secret meeting where the fate of the world was being decided.

There were six strangers sitting around the board game, trying to get to know each other. We rolled the dice and shuffled the pieces around on the board. I had played "Cash Flow" before and was excited to play with some new people. We bought two houses in the board game and then John Mark's phone rang. He got up from the table, took the call quickly in the kitchen, and then returned back to the table.

"Guys, we have a motivated seller on the phone." John Mark smiled as he looked around the table to gauge our interest. "I showed this house today and the Realtor is calling me back saying that his vendor is moving out of town and he's desperate to sell."

Like sharks that had just tasted blood, the six of us, all males, began to surge with testosterone and fantasize about taking advantage of this desperate seller.

"What does he want for the house?" someone asked.

"One hundred and twenty-nine thousand, nine hundred dollars," John Mark replied.

"Let's offer him eighty thousand!" Someone else piped up.

The energy at the table started to rise as the dopamine rush of making money began to release in our minds.

"Let's call him back right now and make an offer! We could buy this right now as a group," someone else said.

The excitement and euphoria of making money was reaching a climax.

"We could buy this house right now; even if we paid a hundred thousand and rented it out for nine hundred a month. We would still make a positive cash flow! We can buy it now in the fall and dump it in the spring when prices go up!" someone else proposed.

We all pulled out our cell phones and began crunching numbers, all at once feeling the rush of buying fake real estate on the board game and now buying a real house at the same time. It was a surreal experience.

"Okay, I'm going to make the call," John Mark suggested.

"We have a power team right here at the table," someone else said.

Sure enough, we had a Realtor, a property manager, and someone who had experience doing their own renovations, and everyone else at the table had owned rental property before. Everyone at the table had some kind of experience with property: everyone except for me.

It seemed like we were all volunteering to pitch in money to buy this house and handle a task. John Mark was the Realtor who would help us buy, someone else was going to manage the property, and someone else was going to crunch the numbers. The deal was coming together right before my eyes and it was coming together fast. I felt the excitement, like I was at a hot table of roulette in Vegas and didn't want to miss out on the action!

"I'll hold the mortgage!" I volunteered, trying to add value to the group; I had no experience, so I figured I could add value by offering my newly minted credit.

"Great!" everyone at the table agreed.

John Mark got out his phone and began negotiating to buy the house. "They want one hundred and twenty-nine thousand, nine hundred dollars… We are going to offer them eighty thousand and see what happens."

"Let's agree to not buy above a hundred thousand," someone suggested.

"Great idea; let's walk away if it goes over $100,000" Everyone at the table agreed and we ended the night excited that we had made a real offer together.

* * *

The following day in the afternoon I got a call from John Mark.

"Congratulations! You just bought a house for one hundred and fifteen thousant dollars!"

"What?" I stammered. "I thought we were going to stop bidding at a hundred thousand!"

"Well, that's what the guy needed to get out of the deal. So we offered him a hundred and fifteen thousand. It's his rock-bottom price."

I suddenly felt sick, because this team I had joined was disorganized and we had already paid more than we agreed to. But still, I wanted to get into real estate so badly that I said, "Alright, let's do it!"

John Mark took me to meet his mortgage broker and rather than getting a mortgage through my branch at the bank, the mortgage broker shopped me around to over 30 different lenders. Since I had a steady paycheck, I was instantly approved. I later met the other five partners at a coffee shop and collected six certified checks of $1,200 each and we had collected enough to put a down payment on our first property.

The deal was crude; we had no real contract, but signed an agreement on a coffee shop napkin that I would hold the title to the property and the mortgage. Everyone owned the house equally, as per the napkin, for one-sixth. I was excited; although I owned only one-sixth of this house, my fear factor was gone and I had finally got my feet wet in the property game.

Within two weeks the possession day came and I picked up the keys. The house was mine. I called my five partners and we met at the house. We brought wine, beer, champagne, and our wives and girlfriends at the time. We celebrated and this was the first time I actually got to see the property. I had bought the house sight unseen and our team was finally examining our purchase. My partners were very pleased with the house, and because they were pleased, I was pleased.

The house had been "flipped" to the vendor in that a property flipper had bought it, fixed it, and sold it to the vendor. The carpet was new, the flooring was new, the paint was new, and the appliances were new. This house would make a perfect rental property.

The property manger in our group said "I'm going to put this property up for rent at nine hundred dollars and see if we have any bites!"

A few days later, I got a call from the manager "Congratulations! We just rented the house for a thousand dollars a month!"

I felt the rush of making money and suddenly thought I was a genius. This house was suddenly the deal of the century. Everyone in the group called one another congratulating each other on being so smart to buy the right house at the right time.

I was an investment genius for three months, and every month I would get a paper statement in the mail along with a rent check. Every month, the property would net after taxes, insurance, principle, and interest $450 a month, and I thought I was the smartest investor in the world.

Finally, on the fourth month, I went to my mother's mailbox to collect the check, and sure enough, there was no check!

I called the manager, but he didn't pick up his phone.

I called everyone else in the group to find out why our cash flow check wasn't coming. "Didn't you hear? The tenants trashed our house and skipped town!" was the grim news I heard from the group.

Our once beautiful investment home had been completely ransacked. The "professional" manager we had hired had paid some tenants $1,000 upfront to take a higher lease for $1,000 a month instead of $900 a month. The higher lease made him look like a hero to the group, but the tenants were poor quality and destroyed the house.

No one could agree on what to do next:

"Lets sell it as is… it's ruined… just sell it!" said one partner.

"Let's fix it ourselves and put in some sweat equity!" said another partner.

"Let's hire someone to fix it up for us," said another partner.

"Let's hire someone to just clean it up and re-rent it damaged," said another.

Some partners didn't care and didn't want to do anything.

I began to feel the stress of being the only one with a direct responsibility for this house. The mortgage was hitting my bank account every month and I didn't have much cash to survive. I got in my car and drove to see the property myself and sure enough, the mailbox was full of court summons, speeding tickets, police business cards, parking tickets, and collections letters.

What kind of animals were we keeping in this house?

The managers had just picked up a few random criminals and rented them my house. As I walked through the front door, I saw beer bottles everywhere, beer-stained carpet, cigarettes burned into the brand-new floor, fist holes punched through walls, doors hacked apart with knives and taken off the hinges, windows smashed, blood on the walls and the floor, and the tenants even left some bloody and used syringes behind.

We had hired a cleaning lady to clean out the house for us, but she quit when she saw the bloody syringes.

I felt angry; I felt stupid. I was in over my head. I called my partners for help, but no one seemed to care enough or agree on a single point of action. The house sat vacant and smashed for weeks while the committee of six argued back and forth over what to do with the house. No one wanted to put in any more money and no one wanted to put in any more time.

Suddenly, I was like a pregnant teenage girl who out of passion had conceived a child. My partners wanted nothing to do with my bastard child and I felt abandoned. It was too late to abandon the baby because I had a mortgage in my name and the word mortgage means "agreement until death." So I rolled up my sleeves and began to fix up, clean, and paint the house myself.

My partners wanted out. They wanted nothing to do with the property and they clearly weren't spending time or money to make the investment a success, so I found one silent partner to buy them out, except for John Mark, who wanted to stay in to help me sell the house when I decided to.

John Mark and I cleaned and painted the house and suddenly I became the property manager. I placed the ads for the tenants, did the interviews, collected the rent, signed the lease, and slowly but surely became responsible for the success of my first investment property.

Stupidity had got me into the deal, and responsibility had bailed me out. I kept the house for five years and then sold it for $169,900.

SELF MADE CONFESSIONS

1. Your best opportunities will always come from the people you know in your network.

2. There is strength and courage by investing in groups, but groups are typically poor at making decisions, there must be a clear and established leader to be successful.

3. When you establish a cutoff price to buy a property, walk away if the seller doesn't meet your price. Don't pay $115,000 for a $100,000 property.

4. Screening tenants and using a legitimate professional property management service is essential to success in investment real estate. When selecting power team members, avoid using friends that you know; they may not be any good and you might have to fire them.

5. Buying property sight unseen is for professionals only—don't try this at home!

6. When stupidity gets you into a situation, responsibility will bail you out every time.

Visit <u>SelfMadeConfessions.com</u> for more lessons.

Confession #19

FOLLOW THE MONEY

"Making money is art and working is art and
good business is the best art."

Andy Warhol

With the confidence of getting my first deal done, I was ready to take over the world. My real-estate investment ship had just sailed her maiden voyage and I was now ready to plunder the seven seas.

John Mark and I had grown close through our experience with my first house and now I was ready to buy more. Somehow, I decided that at the ripe young age of twenty-two, I was ready to quit working forever and ready to enter retirement. I read a book called *How to Retire in One Year* By Robin J. Elliott and decided that retiring in one year was certainly for me. Robin explained that the average North American retires on only $2,000 per month of passive income.

That is enough money for modest living, groceries, transportation, and a few other incidentals. As a guitar teacher and a guy who stocked shelves for a living, a $2,000-a-month passive income sounded like winning the lottery, especially at twenty-two years.

I began to fixate on the number $2,000 per month and scoured the city for a building that would fit my goal. John Mark drove me from building to building, mostly triplexes and fourplexes, and he would help me work out the cash flow on the back of a napkin. Winnipeg was hot at the time and the first building John Mark showed me was a fourplex in an up-and-coming neighborhood. It was the perfect building, and in hindsight I would have made $100,000 in appreciation in one year, but the deal seemed to be easy and I wanted something more creative so I walked away.

The next property I almost bought was a slum rooming house. One of the fastest ways to make a high cash flow in real estate is to buy a large rooming house and rent out each room for $300–$500 per room. John Mark and I went to go look at the same rooming house three times. It was marketed at $149,900 and would make me more than $2,000 a month, but it was located in a dangerous part of town where I would likely get shot or stabbed collecting the rent—Winnipeg is the murder capital of Canada and I didn't want to prove the statistics.

When we went to go see the rooming house for a second look, an old ex-Hells Angels biker showed us the suites; he was the caretaker and also a good warden for the building because he didn't mind fighting. From a lifetime of smoking, this old biker croaked like a frog as he spoke and opened the door to the last unit for us to see. Inside, there was a bare room, like the cell of a prison, with nothing but a filthy bare mattress and a naked middle-aged man with a fat belly like a pig ready to be slaughtered. Although the building would have fit my monetary goals, I wouldn't have been able to live with myself knowing that I owned a piece of hell on earth. Needless to say, although I looked at that rooming house three times, I passed on making an offer.

I wanted to add value to a neighborhood and build something creative. I wanted to be part of a project that had real value. One night at 2 a.m. I was going through my e-mails and then I saw it—the deal I had been looking for!

John Mark had e-mailed me a burned house in an up-and-coming neighborhood. This house was right on the line between the "good" and the "bad" and was just barely on the "bad" side of the neighborhood. It was built in 1902 and was huge compared with other homes in the city at 2,700 square feet and two and a half stories tall. This burned, derelict rooming house was full of mattresses, drugs, abandoned rotting food, pain, misery, and broken lives.

As a rooming house, it was rented out by the room to a medley of drug addicts, prostitutes, refugees from Africa, welfare clients, and other odd characters. But this house was once beautiful and had once been the home of someone powerful, proud, and grand: perhaps a doctor, a lawyer, or a politician.

The address was perfect, it was downtown in Winnipeg, and the neighborhood was rotting at the time, but in five years, it could sense that it would blossom into a hip trendy neighborhood. I was buying ahead of the curve and I knew the location was perfect. The asking price was just reduced from $200,000 down to $159,900 and just from the pictures, I felt that the building should have been worth $350,000, $400,000, or even $450,000 if it were fixed up.

Since it was 2 a.m., it was too early to call John Mark, but I sent him an e-mail that we were going to write an offer that day.

I left my job stocking shelves early to look at the house. The area it was located in was rough, and there were certainly some odd characters living in the area. Across the street from my prospective project were two derelict crack houses full of mattresses and needles. However, I could see that the neighborhood was cleaning up because the local university was investing millions of dollars into the area and the momentum was picking up. One block away, houses had appreciated over $100,000 in one year and I was ready to ride the trend. This crime-ridden block was going to be the next one to turn around and the formula was simple: move out the drug addicts and move in yuppies, DINKs (Double Income No Kids), and students. Buy the derelict houses, fix them, and sell them as cool living spaces in up-and-coming neighborhoods.

I got out of the car with John Mark and we walked around the building. Immediately in my guts, I felt value. The building itself was bigger than any other I had seen, it was cheaper than anything else, and at the back was a downtown parking lot for six cars. I felt as though I had hit the jackpot. Those downtown parking stalls were worth up to $100 per month each and there were six of them. At $600 a month just for parking, I could pay the mortgage on parking alone and leave the house as a burned wreck.

The building itself was in a grotesque state of disrepair. The third floor was completely charred and blackened inside by a fire that had started as an early morning cooking accident. Two people were badly burned in the fire, and the house was wrecked. The second floor had half a dozen soiled mattresses strewn about the floor with rotting food and the walls and floor seemed soggy: the fire hoses that saved the bones of the house had completely wrecked the plaster walls and anything left of the floor.

The first floor was abandoned and had more water damage and more mattresses; the entire building stunk of fire, rotting food, dirty bodies, and money. I wrote an offer that day with John Mark and we began negotiating on the fire-damaged wreck.

I tied up the building at $160,000 with a long six-week due diligence period. The seller accepted my price and gave me lots of time to scramble and find a contractor who could fix up a building that was so badly damaged. It would also give me time to raise the money to buy the building because I had absolutely no cash to fund a project like this. But in my heart, I believed that there was tremendous value to be created and this project would make the perfect investment.

I paid a $1,000 deposit from a credit card to secure the building and suddenly felt the pressure to get to work. I used the skills I had learned to create a loan proposal and business plan. I spent late nights researching the area, coming up with statistics, doing numbers, and building budgets, and finally I had a binder of facts and data that I could show to an investor to build a case for them to fund my crazy project.

The project was indeed crazy. I decided that the third floor of the building was too charred to be saved. My plan was to chop off the third story and build it up another floor. In essence, I was going to take a two-and-a-half-story building and turn it into a full three and a half story. The interior of the building was completely wrecked, so I opted to gut the building, make it open concept, take out the stairs, and change the building from a rooming house for drug addicts into an affordable luxury fourplex for young professionals.

The math was simple: I would buy the building for $160,000, renovate for $150,000, spend $310,000 total, and based on the income, the building would be worth $450,000. From these numbers I figured I could pay my investor a 12% annual return on their cash invested and own a building that could produce $2,000 a month in passive income. Retirement in one year certainly seemed attainable with these numbers.

With my binder complete, I just had to find an investor to fund the project. I needed $10,000 as a down payment to buy the building and at least $150,000 to renovate it. My binder sat on my mother's kitchen table and she noticed I had been working hard on it.

"What's in the binder?" she asked as we passed each other in the kitchen.

"I'm raising money to buy a burned building, fix it up, and rent it out for passive income so I don't need a job ever again," I said nonchalantly.

"That's crazy; I don't want anything to do with that," she said.

Once again, my mother had rejected my real-estate dreams, but I didn't mind at this point. I knew that there were bigger fish in the ocean and that if I stayed at home fishing my own pond, I would never find the fish to get this deal done.

I had heard from a real-estate seminar that doctors and dentists were prime candidates to invest as silent partners in real estate. They a) are high-income earners, b) are bored at their jobs, c) have absolutely no time, and d) are mostly scared to invest alone. By coincidence, I had a dental checkup that afternoon, so I got in the car and went to my appointment.

While I was sitting in the dental chair, my dentist came in to see me and we made some small talk. As he was about to leave, I asked, "Dr. Patel, do you know of anyone who would like to make 12% on their money?"

He paused for a moment, then smiled. "Yes, I know many, mainly me."

"Great," I said. "I have a real-estate deal coming up that would make you twelve percent annually; do you mind if I show you first?"

"Yes!" My dentist smiled feeling as though he had just learned a secret that no one else knew.

My confidence level soared. Although my mother wasn't interested, my dentist was, and the best thing about dentists is that they have more money than teachers.

I carried my binder with me everywhere I could to drum up interest in my real-estate venture. One morning I went for breakfast with my grandmother. Like a cat with a freshly killed bird, I took the binder with me and placed it on the table at breakfast to show off my prize. Grandma was very entrepreneurial and was married to an entrepreneur for her entire life. She asked about the binder immediately and I took her through it like a storybook, explaining the numbers. I showed her the timelines and the facts and figures of the real-estate market. When we got to the end of the binder, she said, "I'll give you ten thousand dollars."

"What?" I couldn't believe it.

"You're paying twelve percent on this deal, I'm getting three percent at the bank, I might as well give my money to you and you can earn me a better return." Grandma smiled and closed the binder. "But there is only one condition…"

"What's that?" I asked.

"Don't tell anyone else in the family. I don't want anyone else to know, or it will seem like I'm playing favorites."

"I won't tell anyone," I said as I looked at her in the eyes and felt the rush of excitement of not only a secret, but also getting to play the game of business again with her grandson after years of idle golf and bridge.

I had raised my first $10,000 for this deal; now I just needed another $150,000 to make my dream a reality.

I went home and placed my binder back on the kitchen table at my mother's house and when she came home from work, she noticed I was excited.

"What are you so excited about?"

"Dr. Patel is interested in investing with me!" I smiled at her, excited about having interest in my deal, but also about being able to move past needing her to actualize my dreams.

"Dr. Patel is interested?" My mother looked at me in disbelief. Suddenly, her crazy son wasn't so crazy.

Value is always seen when more than one person is interested. I could see it in her face; she was uninterested when I had no interest in my project, but suddenly, I had caught the attention of a dentist. She respected the dentist and through my social proof, suddenly saw value.

"And I also have a silent investor who has already committed ten thousand dollars," I whispered as though it was a secret.

"You do?" Her eyes were growing wide and she began to lean in.

Human nature is a wonderful thing. As soon as two people are interested in purchasing something, the value shoots through the roof. Monkey see, monkey do, and when the herd starts to move, our mammalian brains don't want to be left out. My mother leaned back and pursed her lips as she could see the deal of the century blowing past her. Maybe her son actually had something of value? Maybe she was wrong not to invest?

"Sit down," she said. "Show me this deal!"

We sat at the kitchen table and I opened the binder and read it like a storybook to her, much like I had read to my grandmother. When I reached the end of the story where I began to talk about the numbers, I said, "And the building will make two thousand dollars a month in positive cash flow, but you'll get twelve percent annually on your money until the project is done, so if you invest one hundred and fifty thousand dollars and this deal takes six months, you should make nine thousand dollars."

She sat at the table silent for a moment, and then said "I'll give you the money if you split this deal with me... I want to retire, and my pension won't be enough, but I could use an extra thousand dollars per month."

She had entered the kitchen as a lamb, and now I was swimming with a shark. She tasted blood and rather than accepting 12% on her money, she was going for 50% of the deal. My heart raced and my palms sweated; I felt pain behind my face. I pursed my lips and leaned back in my chair. I closed the binder and selfishly said, "Then this deal won't help me reach my goals. I want two thousand a month in passive income, and if I split it with you, I'll only have a thousand!"

I was ready to pack up and call my dentist and shop my deal to other people.

"Wait, let's do this deal together!" suggested my mother. "Let's collaborate; let's be a team. I want to retire; give me half of this deal and help your mom."

I was bleeding to death in the shark-infested waters and I had sat down at the table to pitch her, but the tides had turned and now she was pitching me. I felt anger at giving up half of my venture; I wanted to pay a fixed price for the cash required, but the tender way that she asked me to help her pierced straight to my heart. We both got a little teary-eyed in the moment and neither of us said anything.

"Alright," I said, "let's do it."

We shook hands and after two years of pitching her with no success, I changed her mind. My mother had suddenly become my business partner.

SELF MADE CONFESSIONS

1) You need less to retire than you think; most people retire on $2,000 a month.

2) A few well-purchased investment properties can handle many of your living expenses and free up your time. Triplexes and fourplexes are good candidates for this.

3) Rooming houses, or properties rented out by the room pay some of the highest yield of any investment property, but can also have the most headaches.

4) You make huge gains in property when you buy on the edge of the "good" and "bad" neighborhoods.

5) Areas that are scary today, but will be cool in five years, make great investments. Follow the artists; they are the trendsetters in any city.

6) Your ventures can be packaged into investments for investors to invest in. Make a binder and business plan to sell the dream!

7) Most investors are earning low returns at the bank like 2–3%. If you

can offer them anything higher than that, they will likely invest with you.

8) Value becomes real only when two people become interested. Get two investors interested in your deal and the chances of funding will go up exponentially.

9) You can get anything you want in life if you help enough people get what they want.

Visit <u>SelfMadeConfessions.com</u> for more lessons.

Confession #20

YOUR DREAM CAN
BECOME A NIGHTMARE

"Teamwork makes the dream work, but a vision becomes a
nightmare when the leader has a big dream and a bad team."

JOHN C. MAXWELL

My deal was funded. I had the Money and the Deal; now I just needed the People to magically transform the worst house on the block into the best house in the neighborhood.

John Mark had referred me to a few general contractors and I made many calls. Although I made many calls, only a few contractors agreed to meet me to walk through the building to give me a quote.

The contractor that stood out was Dave. He was twenty-three years old, but had been working on construction sites his whole life. He was a stocky build, average height, drove a huge black pickup truck, and had the demeanor of a battle-hardened warrior. Dave and I walked through the building and he asked me questions about my vision. I painted the broad strokes and asked him to fill in the vision with a detailed quote.

We met at a coffee shop a few days later and he had prepared a quote to chop the roof off the building, build it up one extra floor, gut the entire building, and rebuild the structure as a brand new fourplex. The quote came in at $146,000, which was negotiated down to $136,000. I was happy with the quote because it was far less than $150,000.

It was March and there was still snow on the ground and work wouldn't commence until May. When May rolled around, I quit my job at Frito-Lay to become a full-time developer.

I had quit my job once and failed; I figured that this time it would be different because I had a deal working for me this time. In a few months, it would be finished and I would have cash coming in every month, plus I would do other real-estate deals on the side.

In the beginning, Dave commanded his troops like a four-star general. He stormed the building with a dozen workmen and they ripped the building apart. They tore out the years of rot and decay and stripped the building down to its studs. Once the building was cleaned out, it was beautiful and clean inside. The grand old mansion had ten-foot ceilings and the structure beneath the rot was built out of solid fir. Fir as a wood is superior to the plywood we use on houses today, but is too expensive to use. I felt as though I had hit the jackpot; my deal was funded; I quit my job so I had free time. Dave was working out to be great and nothing was stopping me, until I went to the city to apply for a building permit.

Working with the city administration in any city can be frustrating, but for me, it was excruciating. I had jumped into the real-estate and renovation pool with both feet and suddenly I was drowning in the deep end. The city wanted architectural drawings, stamps, engineer seals, HVAC plans, electrical plans, and plumbing plans, plus I had to apply to have the building rezoned. I was completely unprepared because in my ignorance, I thought I was just fixing up a burned house and not building something new. In the city's eyes, they sent me to the commercial department, who dealt with the construction of brand-new skyscrapers and stadiums. I was way out of my league.

These people were speaking a foreign language to me and no matter how hard I tried, I could not communicate with them. They would ask me for papers, drawings, and seals that I did not know existed. I would ask them what they specifically needed and the asinine answer was always, "I can't tell you." My deal was sailing so smoothly, and suddenly I had smashed up on the rocks. Dave didn't know how to communicate with them and neither did I.

Suddenly, I had a gutted house with no roof, a big mortgage, tons of borrowed money, no job, no building permit, and it rained every day on the bones of my gutted wood house. It was now July and I was running out of money and out of time.

I felt as though I had just stuck my head into a giant garbage compactor and the compressing metal plates were squeezing my eyeballs out. In short, I was stressed. Dave and I both needed the construction to keep going so we could live, so we did what any sensible person would do: we kept the renovations going as per our plans without a permit. I showed up at the city every day and tried my best to communicate with them while construction took place, but my presence started to aggravate them, and this made the permit process even more painful.

Eventually, my lack of income forced me to get another job, and this time I was hired by the company selling private equity and investments. I had quit my job twice now and failed to be a real entrepreneur twice, but just like in baseball, the players who strike out the most also hit the most home runs.

My construction project was supposed to be six months, as Dave quoted me. It was supposed to be easy, in and out. After all, it was not rocket science, just simple construction. Overnight, my dream of a project suddenly turned into a nightmare. The project was a beast, far too big and far too complicated.

With menacing jaws, the project began to eat me alive.

My six-month project suddenly ballooned into an 18-month hell ride. Demanding cash calls were attacking me from every direction and the unexpected costs and construction overruns began to pile up. The budget that had once been $150,000 quickly expanded into $250,000. The extra $100,000 was absorbed by my credit cards, my mother's credit cards, lines of credit, and 0% credit accounts from three different hardware stores. The debt and the leverage that I committed to the project squeezed me so hard I felt sick when I thought about it. Because it made me sick, most days, I didn't think about it.

I called Dave every day to check in on the project and every day he told me that things were slowly moving along. He knew what I wanted to hear and fed what I wanted instead of the cruel reality. Most people prefer comforting lies to uncomfortable truths and he fed me enough comforting lies to build a very comfortable bed to lie down and die in.

Dave's crew had started with a dozen hearty workmen swinging hammers and sledge hammers that were working fast like storm troopers blitzing enemy territory and now, nearly a year later, it was only Dave left and a few tired toothless drunks who shuffled around in the bowels of my building.

I was pious; I was prideful; I was sitting in my comfortable, heated investment office at the private equity firm in my perfectly tailored suit while Dave and his toothless soldiers suffered in the dead of winter. The project was not going well, but instead of rolling up my sleeves and getting more hands on, I became more hands off. The music Dave's band was playing was not the music I wanted to hear, so I stuck my head in the sand and hoped it would all go away.

Things were not going well at the private equity firm either. When I had volunteered for the company, they promised a return of 20% annually to their customers. When I was hired, it became 15%. When I got into the field and started selling, it was 6–8%. When I was training other salesmen, it was 5%. When I left the company 10 months later, it was 3%, and after I left, it became 2%. Something strange was happening in the leadership and management of the company.

I wasn't sure if the loss of returns was due to crooks or clowns, but the company was not selling as well as it used to. The pressure in the company made the managers tighten their grip on the sales force like a master disciplining a badly behaved dog. Very quickly, almost in a flash, my vacuum sales mentors were gone from the company along with most of the top talent. What was once arguably the best money-raising team in the country was disbanded in a matter of six months. I began to hear rumors in the ranks of the salespeople all across the country that the investments we were raising for were unsound. Some of the deals were failing and the management was supposedly using good deals to bail out the bad deals. The securities commission smelled blood and was sniffing around and auditing the company every month. The tension continued to mount like a guitar string that had been strung too tightly. Finally, I heard a rumor that one of the men we were raising money for was a child pornographer and I didn't know if this was true or not, but the tension of my guitar string snapped.

Even rats know when to jump off a sinking ship, and the turmoil inside the organization plus the drama and loss of so many good salespeople completely extinguished my appetite to work there. The phone that I used to dial 50 times every day suddenly felt as though it weighed ten thousand pounds. In my last weeks at the company, I sat in my chair and made no calls. Instead of high energy, enthusiasm, and excitement pumping through the office, the sounds of selling were replaced by the deafening roar of silence. All I did was stare out the window by my desk at the Canadian prairie trains silently rolling back and forth behind the office. I would stare at those trains for hours and do nothing. Every day I came to work and all sound was on mute while I watched the trains.

Finally, I picked up the phone and called the owner of the company myself and quit. My contract stated I could quit at anytime with no notice and I could be fired at anytime with no notice. I honored my contract and called the owner like a man, rather than hiding behind the human resources department. I destroyed all the evidence I had ever been there, cleaned out the desk, and closed the door forever.

I came home to my mother's kitchen table and as she walked in from work, she saw me sitting at the table in my suit. "Why are you home so early?" she asked.

"I quit my job today," I said, looking at her with pain in my face, but also with a glimmer of hope.

"You what?" she hissed at me, lashing venom from between her lips.

"I quit my job today," I said as I got up from my chair and went up to my room to take my suit off.

When I came back downstairs dressed in shorts and a T-shirt, sitting at my kitchen table were my mother, my grandmother, and my brother.

"Sit down!" commanded my mother. "We are having an intervention."

I sat down.

"What the hell do you think you're doing?" she continued. "What is going on with this house we are renovating? It's taking forever and it's bleeding me dry! I'm so stressed, my credit cards are maxed, my lines of credit are maxed, and I can't sleep! And then you decide to quit your job; what the hell? You are just like your father!"

Her words stung me like a harpoon pierces the belly of a whale. The words "You are just like your father" was the killing blow, and flashes of pain surged through my body. Grandma and my brother were silent, but they looked at me with concern. I was like an alcoholic who had been caught sprawled out in the gutter one too many times. Except, instead of drinking as an addiction, I had a fantasy business addiction. Here I was, lying in the filth of my waste, drunk on my dreams and repenting for my sins.

"You need to put on your old painting clothes and go down there every day and work on the house yourself until it's finished! It's time to take some responsibility for your life and for my money and finish this damn project off before it kills us all!" commanded my mother. Her words were motivating, angry, and scared. They stirred my guts like a witch's brew.

"OK," I said, feeling ashamed of myself. "I'll do whatever it takes to get this thing done." All the four of us were silent at the table for a moment, and then I pushed my chair out and went upstairs to my room.

I logged into my online bank account and surveyed my financial situation. All of my credit cards were maxed out and all of my lines of credit were pushed to the limit. I had two mortgages, a car loan, and only a few thousand dollars in my checking account. I had no job, and no income. In 90 days I would be bankrupt and financially dead if I didn't get this deal finished. Worse off, my mother would also be bankrupt and we would lose our home. This venture was no longer a matter of pride, it was now a matter of life and death.

SELF MADE LESSONS

1. Always get three quotes from three independent contractors. Three quotes is the magic number.

2. Dealing with the city administration is best left to the professionals.

You want to communicate through professional builders, professional architects, and professional engineers.

3. A professional contractor will get all of the permits necessary to handle your project. If your contractor is scared of the city, then he is not a professional.

4. When key company players, officers, and consultants begin to quit, it's an early sign that the company is in trouble.

5. When a renovation project is dragging on for double or triple time, it's time to roll up your sleeves and take command rather than pull away.

6. Taking full responsibility for a mess will almost always cure a situation caused by irresponsibility.

Visit <u>SelfMadeConfessions.com</u> for more lessons.

Confession #21

SAVAGES GET RESULTS

"Problem solving is hunting.
It is savage pleasure and we are born to it."

THOMAS HARRIS

All my life I had been a person with too many options. Perhaps I received too many gifts at birth or too many curiosities and interests. I could never find the one thing to focus on. Now that my entire life, and not just my life, but also my mother's life was on the line, I suddenly had no options. Every morning when I woke up, all I could think of was finishing off my deal, and every night all I could think about when I went to bed was finishing off my deal.

Although it was stressful to an outside observer, I entered a calm bliss as my once-noisy mind full of backtalk and self-doubt suddenly went silent while I served my one and only purpose—finish off this house or die.

I had 90 days to live and then the music would stop. In the game of musical chairs, I knew that I would be stuck without a chair. Losing this game was not an option, because unlike a game, I could not afford to fail or make any more mistakes. I began to feel like my situation, and perhaps the house was cursed. My house had burned and people were badly disfigured in the fire. Perhaps their spirits were lingering?

Out of superstition, and a feeling of total helplessness and oblivion, I had the half-finished house exorcised from ghosts and blessed by a priest. I was not a religious person by nature, but I suddenly felt small and insignificant relative to my problems that could crush me at any moment. It was a miracle the house didn't burn down because I didn't even have proper insurance without a full building permit. Since I had made it this far, I felt as though there was a force either protecting me or damning me. At this point, I wanted to do anything to get on the force's good side.

My father once told me that it takes seven compounded mistakes to crash a plane. One or two mistakes and the pilot can recover, but once the pilot makes seven compound mistakes, recovery becomes impossible. I had made far too many mistakes on this project and it was nose-diving straight into the ground. If I didn't act fast, I was going to crash and burn alive in the flames.

I put my perfectly tailored suits away in the closet and closed the door on them; I knew I wouldn't need them where I was going. Instead of a suit, each day I wore my white painter pants that I had worn for four summers and had painted hundreds of houses in.

The pants used to be white, but they were now a rainbow mosaic of neutral grays, pinks, greens, and tans that most homeowners preferred for their homes. I didn't wear a shirt, because I didn't deserve one, so I wore an unzipped painter jacket that showed off my bare chest like a savage warrior. I felt like a warrior, but looked like a homeless man. The jacket was also splattered in paint from projects completed in the past and as I painted more projects, my chest became christened with war paint as well. I gave up on combing my hair and let it run wild in rebellion against the world. I didn't bother to shave my face as dark stubble replaced my clean-shaven aesthetic and the shadow on my chin matched the shadows of my dark sunken eyes. I looked like a savage from a war-torn jungle that killed his enemies in cold blood and took no prisoners. I was once civilized, but savage I became. The time for prisoners was over and I was ready to become the merciless warlord of my battlefield and take full responsibility for victory or defeat.

I rolled up to my half-built mess and stepped out of the car. My steel-toed boots crushed the gravel beneath my step. Dave and his toothless helpers all stopped moving and looked at me in disbelief. The slick man who showed up every day in a suit had showed up shirtless, covered in war paint, with wild savage hair, dark stubble, and dark circles under his eyes.

His gaze from the dark sunken sockets in his skull was piercing, focused, and determined. The man in the suit was dead; his incompetence had killed him. Now they had to live with the man's insane alter ego.

"I'm in charge now," I said coldly as I surveyed the battlefield.

Everything on the construction site was a half-done: half-done paint, half-done soffits, half-done carpentry, half-done roof, half-done windows, half-done kitchens—everything was half-done! Materials and garbage were comingled into piles strewn about the wreckage. Tools were disorganized, littered, and forgotten everywhere. Dave's face had grown fat with worry; he pursed his lips so tightly that his face resembled an anus.

His mouth was the center of the anus, which was fitting because everything he said was BS. When I met him, he was stocky, but now he had gained weight under stress and looked like a fat lazy pig. He had also stopped taking action on nearly everything and vomited a series of excuses for why things weren't done. Although he didn't say it, I felt as though he had given up and chosen to die in my project.

"What do we need?" I barked.

"Materials," replied Dave.

"Why don't we have them?"

"No money." Dave looked at the ground.

He had lived off my money for too many months and no longer had money to finish the project. Blindly, I had given him money for construction and in my ignorance, failed to track what he was spending it on. The money that was supposed to paint my walls was instead feeding his fattened face and going straight into his belly.

"OK," I hissed. "Get in my car; we are going to the hardware store to pick up materials."

"But we have no money," objected Dave.

"Get in the car, I'll handle it." So I took Dave to five different hardware stores, where he picked out the materials he needed. I opened another credit account to pay for them.

"My truck broke months ago and I had no money to fix it," objected Dave. "We can't even move this stuff to the project..."

"Get me some bungee cords and plastic flags and we'll put it in my car!" I ordered. My patience with Dave was getting short, but he had already spent my money, so he became my guilty prisoner. I had grown to hate him, but I had to keep him around and alive long enough until the project was done.

We loaded my small four-door sedan illegally with toilets, vanities, lumber, doors, doorframes, baseboards, trim, and anything else the house required. I tied orange plastic flags onto pieces that stuck out the windows. I drove with my trunk wide open and made sure I took the back lanes to avoid the police from giving me a ticket. Dave's band of criminals had robbed me and now I was one of them, breaking all the rules and slithering in the shadows to survive.

As I delivered the materials, I started to make lists of every task that had to be done to finish the suites one by one. Each list was taped to the back of the suite door and Dave's drunks were assigned to finish off each specific piece. Dave had no materials and I solved his problem, but his next problem was people. His band of criminals had no teeth and no skills to do the finishing on the project. Worse off, he fired every single person I brought on to help him.

Dave refused to pay anyone more than $15 per hour for labor, and the type of finishing carpenter he needed was a minimum of $30 per hour. The way Dave was thinking, this problem was impossible to solve.

Immediately I got out my phone and began calling everyone I knew. I also called through the online classifieds, looking for labor. In the end, I hired three extra contractors to finish off the house and within 45 days, the entire project was completed right in front of Dave's face while he sulked around and watched his half-done failure finish without him.

The pressure that had squeezed my head every night and had kept my mother from sleeping was almost gone. Once we filled the suites and leased out the whole building, cash started to trickle in. Watching the cash flow in was like breathing through a straw after running out of oxygen. It was one of the best feelings in the world. Midway through the project I had refinanced the property with the bank and now that it was complete, I was entitled to $100,000 in cash to repay my mother and other creditors for construction expenses.

As I walked into the bank to claim my $100,000 check, the banker looked at me and said, "I'm sorry, I can't give you your check… Someone has put a construction lien on your project and the bank won't advance any funds until it's lifted!"

I wished the banker had hit me with a shovel instead. I went home to my mother's house and opened the mail. Inside was a letter informing me that Dave had put a lien on my project for $75,000 and claimed that I owed him the money for work he completed!

Criminals are always criminals and the sad part is that $75,000 was the remainder of his construction contract that he never fulfilled. I hired three other contractors to tie up his loose ends and paid those contractors accordingly. In actual fact, Dave was entitled to $0 for not completing the project, but being the snake he was, he struck me with one final bite of venom before I put him back in the grass.

I called my lawyer and weighed out the options. Dave knew the money wasn't his, and I knew the money wasn't his, but I needed the $100,000 to pay out the credit cards and lines of credit that were strangling my mother and me. I was between a rock and a hard place, and Dave knew it. There were two options: 1) go to court, litigate, and burn money like paper or 2) pay Dave a "go away" settlement.

The magic number to make the snake go away was $25,000, and I paid his ransom begrudgingly. "This isn't justice, but it's business," said my lawyer with a smile as I handed him the check with a clenched fist.

The $100,000 check came promptly from the bank and most of my debts were settled, along with all of my mother's high-interest debts. Cash flow came in every month from day one of completion, and although it took 18 months and cost $450,000 in total to build, the building turned out better than we anticipated and is now worth close to $600,000 with a gross income of roughly $55,000 a year. In effect, the income was like having another family member who worked full-time and gave up all of their earnings. Pressure makes diamonds and although the numbers worked out well on the project, blood, sweat, and tears that I invested paid me the greatest dividends of all. I had entered financial hell and survived a near-death financial experience. I was now a survivor, hardened by battle, and knew what it took to slither with the snakes and survive in real estate.

SELF MADE LESSONS

1. Having too many options in today's world is a curse that too many people have. Having no options is a luxury because it forces a mind to focus.

2. The mark of a true leader is the ability to roll up his sleeves and step into the trenches when his team is failing.

3. Never give your contractors too much cash; always track and verify that they are spending your money on your project.

4. Never allow a toothless contractor onto your jobsite. If he can't take care of his own teeth, he can't take care of your project.

Visit SelfMadeConfessions.com for more lessons.

Confession #22

CAN YOU SMELL THE MONEY?

"The lack of money is the root of all evil."

MARK TWAIN

Working at the private equity firm had some perks. Although I worked from 10 a.m. to 10 p.m. Monday to Friday and most Saturdays, there were some fringe benefits. One of the best benefits was the local visibility through public speaking and having an aura of local celebrity.

I was speaking at a local Winnipeg event for the private equity firm and after the presentation, an old man in his sixties approached me from the audience.

"Do you do real-estate joint ventures?" he asked as he breathed a cloud of the worst-smelling breath imaginable into my face.

"Yes!" I said, choking on the bitter smell of his breath.

"I have a deal and I'm looking for funding; let me tell you more."

His name was Gary and he was an old wantrepreneur who worked security at night and collected and sold used watches during the day. He was dirty, smelly, had long white hair, a white moustache, and big bifocal glasses that were probably cool in the 1970s. He wore a plaid jacket like a university professor; apparently he had three university degrees to go with the jacket. Everything about him was shabby.

I agreed to meet him at his deal later that week. I showed up to his address at one of the most desirable rental addresses in town and out front of a 1970s side-by-side duplex was Gary. Gary took me inside his unit and showed me around. He was a hoarder and his entire suite was full of junk. His suite had the exact same rotten stench that his breath had and the smell seemed to be seeping in from the dirty stained walls.

The roof was leaking and nothing had been updated since 1970 when the duplex was built. I knew Gary was crazy when I went upstairs to look in one of his bedrooms and the entire room was full of dirty watches that he hoarded over the years and in the next room was a dirty mattress that stunk like his breath.

If I was new to real estate, I would have gagged on the smell, but I had a few deals under my belt, so I knew that this building smelled like money.

Gary had been living in the suite for years and was renting with a roommate. He fancied himself as a real-estate aficionado so had tried to negotiate the purchase of the building with the owner, named Ferd, but Gary had no money and no ability to borrow.

Ferd was an old, retired, successful Realtor who owned many buildings around the city and wanted to let go of them. Ferd was willing to sell the building to Gary for only $10,000 down and he would carry the rest of the $225,000 building as a vendor take-back mortgage so no banks were involved. I'm not sure if Gary or Ferd knew, but the building was easily worth more than $400,000 fixed up.

This situation was the holy grail of real-estate investments: it had a creative, reasonable vendor, an ugly building at half price, and a great location!

I had Gary call Ferd and when he came over, immediately, very quickly, on the spot, Ferd and I were striking a deal to buy the property. Gary glared at me jealously as I pulled out a purchase contract from my car and we started writing the contract. As quickly as the ink dried, I was on the phone to John Mark, my Realtor and I began to ask him what a building like Ferd's would sell for. "Why do you ask?" asked John Mark.

"I have this building tied up and I think I'm going to flip it," I replied.

"Are you looking for investors?" asked John Mark. "I'm in!"

I hadn't even asked for the money and already, because the deal was so good, John Mark was wiling to supply all of the cash to buy and fix up the property. He had done very well on another deal and had over $100,000 to invest.

"OK, sounds good!" I said. "Come take a look."

John Mark drove down immediately and we looked at the building; we both agreed it was a great purchase and shook hands with Ferd. As Ferd drove off in his pickup truck, Gary came out in front of the building to confront us and he was angry. "What do I get out of this deal?" he demanded. "This is my deal!"

"Gary, you can't bring anything to the table on this one; I'll take care of you." I raised my hand like a Jedi master telling Gary to calm down. "I'll give you some money," I said under my breath and Gary slithered away.

We went to his office and examined the comparables. A premium duplex would sell for up to $420,000 and I had it under contract for only $225,000 with Ferd financing most of the purchase instead of the bank!

Very quickly, we closed on the property and weeks before closing I received daily calls from Gary. "Where's my money?" he demanded.

"You get your money when we close," I defended. Each day, Gary got crazier and more aggressive.

Finally on the day of closing, John Mark and I showed up to the duplex and Gary refused to get out of his unit. I had a $5,000 check with his name on it that I was willing to pay as a finder's fee for such a great deal. Unfortunately, the whole situation escalated into an NYPD hostage negotiation.

Gary refused to leave his house because he was so scared of getting ripped off by John Mark and me. On our side, we refused to give him the check unless he got out. To make matters worse, Gary had already spent the $5,000 I was going to give him on a camping trailer and apparently was starting to pay interest on the trailer loan. The lack of money, the root of all evil, was stressing him out. Finally, Gary's wife, a sweet, blonde, short European lady, came into the negotiation and calmed Gary down. She was like a snake charmer who had calmed down a viscous cobra and lured him out of the house. I handed Gary his check in good faith that he would bring more deals in the future. I never saw him again.

Since I was working at the private equity firm at the time, and still had a good relationship with Dave (my bad contractor), I figured we would hire him to renovate the duplex because I trusted him at the time of purchase.

This duplex was supposed to take six months and after a few months, I quit the private equity firm to force Dave to finish my fourplex. Unfortunately, I had to fire him from the duplex halfway through the job because of our disputes over my fourplex. Somehow, by accident, I became the general contractor and showed up the jobsite every day in my warlord costume.

Compared with my burned house, this duplex was a cakewalk. Everything was cosmetic, which meant everything was profitable. I managed a small band of contractors and had the building painted inside and out. Ironically, one of the painters was my old summertime employer when I was nineteen years old and now at twenty-three I was employing him. He looked at me with disbelief as I hired him for the job to flip my real estate. When I was nineteen, I was a punk rock musician with long hair that he hired to paint schools in the summer and now I was a mini-real-estate mogul flipping houses with none of my own money.

As well as paint, we had the flooring redone, two kitchens installed, the roof repaired, and the basements cleaned up and finished. The project ran a little over budget, as I didn't really have my footing yet with doing the most efficient renovations, but six months after purchase for $225,000, we sold the building with cash-flowing leases for $408,000 for a total of $183,000 more than we bought it for!

With the profits from this deal, I wiped out all of my credit cards and became debt-free. Finally, I had no debt and no job. It was time to do more deals!

SELF MADE LESSONS

1. Public speaking is one of the fastest ways to increase your influence and your income.

2. Strange people often have strange houses to sell.

3. If the house stinks, don't be alarmed. Stinky is the smell of money.

4. Vendors who are retiring and own their buildings free and clear love to sell their buildings and hold a vendor take-back mortgage. These are more common than you think, ask and ye shall receive.

5. Always pay those who refer you deals. You never know when they will bring you the next great deal.

6. Never give a contractor more work than he can handle; he won't get it done!

7. Cosmetic renovations, namely kitchens, bathrooms, flooring, and paint are the most profitable renovations for any property.

Visit SelfMadeConfessions.com for more lessons.

Confession #23

YOUR LAST $500

"I have no money, no resources, no hopes.
I am the happiest man alive."

HENRY MILLER

I had made it out of the jaws of the beast alive. My first deal was sta-
bilized and cash flowing, then my fourplex nearly killed me but was
finally stable and bringing in monthly cash. I had flipped Ferd's duplex for
profit and suddenly had no debt but also no job and no earned income.

The small income I made on my cash-flowing real estate was enough
money to live the dream of lying around at Mom's house, playing video
games for the rest of my life. But that didn't suit me. They say that ships
are safest in harbor, but ships are meant for sailing. I had an appetite for
adventure.

I had quit my job three times so far in my life. The first two times I had
failed because I didn't have the experience or the business acumen to survive. The third time I quit my job was going to be my final and perma-
nent launch into entrepreneurship. I knew I had earned the right to be an
entrepreneur because I knew how to sell well enough to support myself
on sales commissions alone. I had proved myself as a money-raising machine for real estate by raising over $1,100,000 in 10 months for the pri-
vate equity firm, and I also had a few deals under my belt. It was time to
go full-time into the jungle of real-estate investing and never look back.

I made a crude business plan on the back of a napkin and very simply, my plan was to buy one house per month with a joint venture partner. The partner would supply all the cash to purchase and get a mortgage. The house would make a gross cash flow of $450 per month. After I charged the deal management fees, which I would take of roughly $100 per month, I would also take a profit of roughly $100 per month.

If I did one house per month for the next five years (or 60 months), I would have $6,000 per month in profits (assuming $100 per door) and $6,000 per month in management fees. The plan seemed perfect in theory and I got to work creating a real business plan and binder.

Very quickly, I called up my Realtor, John Mark, and let him know of my plan. He liked the idea, so I began finding undervalued houses in Winnipeg. I was buying mostly on the MLS or Multiple Listing Service, so typically, you would have to look at 100 houses, write 10 offers, get 3 accepted, and close on 1 deal. John Mark and I looked at hundreds of houses and drove around town, writing aggressively low offers.

Over the next six months, I had acquired and filled six cash-flowing houses with a handful of investors backing me. The job was grueling and required super-human endurance by the time I got to six houses because house #1 would still have management problems to take care of while I was trying to rent out house #6. Plus I was trying to buy house #7 and find more investors for house #8, #9, and #10.

I was working 18 hours a day and almost reached my breaking point; worse off, the houses began to have tenant problems and surprises that would cash call me and I began to absorb some of the cash calls onto my credit cards to avoid spending any cash. My house of cards and my brilliant plan were starting to crumble as the responsibilities were getting too big for my one-man show. I had to manage not only my growing real-estate business, but also my other rental units. Suddenly, I hit a magic number. I now had more than ten rental units and self-management was becoming a nightmare.

I now had more money and more problems. The cash calls began to spiral out of control and the cash management became more and more difficult. My plan was half working: investors wanted to invest with me and I was finding houses. However, my plan was failing because the actual numbers achieved were not matching my projections.

I started to feel lost and began to jump back into real-estate seminars on credit cards to find some answers. I had attended many seminars in the past and now had some experience in doing deals. I was making small amounts of money, but didn't know how to run my real estate like a business.

I had maxed out my credit cards on seminars in the past and was not interested in doing it again, but I felt like I only had half the story. I knew how to do deals, I knew how to raise money, but I didn't know how to make a living and a lifestyle off of real estate. The gurus had advertised a dream of freedom and living on beaches; how could I achieve that in my current situation? Between living, seminars, travel to seminars, cash calls, and other small business investments, my clear credit cards had suddenly become nearly maxed again. Who knew that starting a full-time real-estate investment business was so expensive?

From one of the seminars I learned to place "We Buy Houses" ads in the online classifieds. I started to learn little bits and pieces of marketing and other business skills that I was lacking. Like a bird building a nest, I took every little twig and piece of dirt and slowly built a functioning foundation.

I placed a "We Buy Houses" ad online and very quickly, almost too quickly, my phone rang.

"Hello?" I said into the receiver.

"Hi, do you buy houses?" asked a young female voice.

"Uhhhh…. Yes? I do." I replied sounding unsure of myself.

"OK, can you come take a look at my house? I want to sell it," said the lady in an uncomfortable voice.

The entire call was awkward, but I learned that her name was Jane and that she had recently inherited her uncle's house. Her uncle was an old World War II veteran who was also a hoarder and filled his small 1940s bungalow up to the rafters with guns, old furniture, and dead deer heads. The entire house smelled like cat pee because apparently the uncle had cared for cats, and the garage was full of guns and junk as well. The yard looked like a jungle with weeds growing six feet tall in the front and back; the whole house appeared to be abandoned.

The saving grace with this house was the fact that it was located in a great part of town—a high-demand area with good schools that everyone wanted to live at. I rolled up to the address, and out front sat Jane and her brother.

Jane and her brother were doing their best to clean out their dead uncle's house. The smell of cat pee was making them gag, but to me, I only smelled money. I knew right away that this house was worth at least $160,000 and wondered what they were asking for the house.

"We've got some other people coming to look at it later," she mentioned. Jane looked like an innocent lamb, but she was a vicious wolf when it came to negotiating. She put pressure on me right away.

I walked through the house and my feet felt sticky walking over the cat-pee-stained floors. I pulled out a napkin and did some quick numbers. By my calculations, I would invest roughly $20,000 to fix the house up, so I could pay up to $100,000 for the house and still make a modest profit.

"I can pay you eighty thousand dollars," I said coldly to Jane as if I didn't want the house.

"OK, we'll think about it," she replied and I got back in my car and drove away.

Later that evening, she called me back and said, "We want a hundred thousand, and someone else offered us a hundred thousand. If you pay a hundred thousand, then we have a deal. If not, then we'll sell to the other guy." Jane was a shrewd negotiator with her "take it or leave it" attitude. I wasn't sure if she had another guy, but I didn't want to call her bluff because even at $100,000 it was a good deal.

"OK," I said, "Let's do $100,000."

I got off the phone and called John Mark again, like clockwork; he was in for this deal too. We financed the deal with a hard moneylender and John Mark picked up the rest of renovations. I became the manager of the deal and by this time I had a proven contracting crew that could handle the entire project from the cradle to the grave.

By this time, I was getting frustrated with my business model. My buy-and-hold deals were cash calling me and slowly eating up my credit cards. Worse off, the cash they brought in was peanuts compared with my mounting expenses. I had no steady income, no time, and no job. I had the sales skills and the ability to do deals, which served me well as an investor, but I was lost when it came to running a full-time real-estate business. I had no one to look up to or ask for help. Who did I know who could help me? No one that I knew. Every investor I knew of had a part-time job, or was a Realtor. As far as I knew, full-time pure real-estate investors were like unicorns—very rare.

Dissatisfied with my position, I flew to Las Vegas for a real-estate investor convention. Going to the United States was a whole different world. When you compare business in Canada with business in the USA, everything is bigger and better in America. I watched speakers for three days from around the world practicing different types of real-estate investment. Each and every one of these gurus had an amazing story and each one had a unique strategy. Finally, I saw a young man of about thirty-two years of age get up on stage. He claimed that he had done 500 deals since the age of twenty-three and as soon as I heard the word *five hundred,* I was hooked.

That year I was going to do 12 deals; how could this man do 500 deals before the age of thirty-two? The number 500 mesmerized me. I did the math in my head to compute that kind of real-estate business, but it blew my mind.

As he got off stage, I met him in person and said, "I want to do five hundred deals too! How did you do it?"

He looked at me quickly, scanned me, and saw that I was serious. "Let's go have lunch."

At lunch, he pulled out a napkin and drew the entire business model out for me. It was brilliant and I wanted to replicate it, and I also wanted to know more.

"I've got to go, but you can have this napkin," he said as he got up to leave.

"I need help implementing this!" I stammered. "Can you help me?"

He had already turned to leave, but looked at me over his shoulder. "I would love to, but I simply don't have any time. I help my serious coaching students only." He started to walk away.

"Wait!" I said, feeling desperate. "What does it take to be a student?"

"Ten thousand dollars and you get four phone calls and we'll spend a day together."

"Ten thousand dollars?" I choked. I couldn't believe the price, but I also couldn't pass up the opportunity. I needed to learn the business from someone who had done it and this guy was the perfect candidate. "I can do a five-hundred-dollar deposit right now on my Visa!"

"OK," he said as he jotted down my Visa number on a napkin. "I'll call my office and have them run this; once you pay the rest, we can get started." With that, he stuffed the napkin in his pocket and turned to leave.

I was relieved and scared all at the same time. I needed to know what this man knew. His knowledge and expertise could take my business to the next level. But at the same time, $10,000 was a lot of money and I didn't have access to that amount of cash.

When I got home to Winnipeg, I checked my credit card balances: maxed, maxed, maxed.

Once again, I had no cash and no credit and the $500 I had paid the guru was the last $500 of room I had available on any of my credit cards.

I wanted to cry. I had a clear vision of who I needed to help me, but fear, worry, and doubt began to set in. My maxed credit cards were stopping me from moving ahead with my career and I was frustrated.

I picked up the phone to call the guru for my $500 back. I left a voicemail; no response.

I sent him an e-mail asking for my $500 back because I couldn't follow through with the program: still no response.

I left many more voicemails and many more e-mails pleading for my $500 and still no response. He was either a crook, or he was teaching me a lesson.

My crew was finishing off the house I bought from Jane and we were getting it ready for sale. The house looked stunning, like a mini show home and I was able to sell it privately within a week for $172,000, even more than I had planned at $160,000. Plus since I sold it privately, I saved the Realtor commission.

We had bought the house for $100,000, planned to sell it for $160,000, and sold it thirty days after purchasing it for $172,000. We sold it for $72,000 more than we bought it for! This was the fastest flip I had ever done! The cash I made was a shot in the arm and enough to fulfill my napkin contract with the guru. He wasn't answering his phone, but I knew that he was giving me some tough love.

Real winners don't back out of their agreements even if they are written on napkins, and he wasn't going to back out. I sent him an e-mail letting him know that I was ready to follow through on my contract and quickly received a reply. A single line that read:

"Fly to Chicago."

I booked my ticket and was ready to learn from the master.

SELF MADE LESSONS

1. Don't quit your job to be an entrepreneur until you are proficient at selling. Proficient means the best on the sales team and earning more than $100,000 per year.

2. When buying houses on the MLS in your market, obey the 100:10:3:1 rule. Look at 100, write offers on 10, 3 are accepted, 1 is acceptable.

3. Any small property (aka 4 units or less) will not truly cash-flow if there is more than a 50% debt to equity ratio.

4. Being able to do one or two real-estate deals successfully and building a business of doing deals are two different things: The first requires re-

al-estate knowledge; the second requires knowledge of entrepreneur-ship.

5. Some of the best deals come from "We Buy Houses" signs and online ads.

6. When dealing with private sellers, force them to make a deal on the spot. "I'll think about it" means that other buyers are coming to outbid you. Don't let that happen.

7. Hard money lenders are private people who lend to real-estate inves-tors at high interest rates. You can expect to pay 9–18% in interest and 2–5% in upfront fees, but the access to the money is usually worth the cost.

8. There are only three ways to get ahead in life: 1) The blood, sweat, and tears method, aka trial and error (the slow and expensive way). 2) Work for free (the slow and cheap way). 3) Find someone who has achieved what you want and pay them for an accelerated education. (The fastest and cheapest way in the long run.)

Visit <u>SelfMadeConfessions.com</u> for more lessons.

Part 2

THE 5 SECRETS THAT TRANSFORM ORDINARY PEOPLE INTO SELF MADE MILLIONAIRES

WELCOME TO THE JUNGLE

"The trading floor is a jungle… and the guy you end up working for is your jungle leader. Whether you succeed here or not depends on knowing how to survive in the jungle. You've got to learn from your boss. He's key. Imagine if I take two people and I put them in the middle of the jungle and I give one person a jungle guide and the other person nothing. Inside the jungle there's a lot of bad shit going down. Outside the jungle there's a TV that's got the NCAA finals on and a huge fridge full of Bud… chances are good that the guy with the jungle guide is gonna be the first one through the jungle to the TV and the beer. Not to say the other guy won't eventually get there too. But… he'll be reeeaaal thirsty and there's not going to be any beer left when he arrives."

—MICHAEL LEWIS, *LIAR'S POKER*

Confession #24

WELCOME TO THE JUNGLE

"Deep into that darkness peering, long I stood there,
wondering, fearing, doubting, dreaming dreams no
mortal ever dared to dream before."

EDGAR ALLAN POE

I flew into Chicago in November and took a cab to the airport hotel. My ribs were shaking with excitement or maybe fear because I knew my life was about to change.

In life, we typically have two great fears: one is the fear of failure and the other is the fear of success. Ironically, fear of success is much more frightening because it destroys who you once were and brings change. Every human being on the planet fears change. I had achieved some success in real estate and made some money but had also made some very painful mistakes along the way. I knew how to raise money, I knew how to write a business plan for a single deal, but I couldn't figure out how to put together a self-sustaining business model of real estate that would support me and eventually make me rich.

My phone buzzed in my pocket and I pulled it out. A text from the guru read, "Front entrance, black Escalade."

I rode the elevator downstairs and walked through the glass sliding doors of the hotel entrance. Out front was a shiny huge black escalade and inside was the guru wearing sunglasses and golf clothes.

I opened the passenger door and climbed in.

"Welcome to the Jungle," he said with a grin. "I didn't think you were going to make it; most people don't. Everyone has big dreams, but few people are committed enough to invest in themselves and see their dreams through to fruition. Congratulations for taking the first step."

"Thanks." I gulped, not sure if I had made the right choice.

They say that the difference between crazy people and eccentric people is money. If he didn't have money, I would have got up and left. But instead, I reached into my briefcase and pulled out a certified check for $9,500 and handed it to him, finalizing our napkin contract we had made when we met. To an outsider our transaction could have looked like a drug deal or some other type of organized crime: two guys exchanging a sizable check in a black Escalade; but in reality, most business deals are made with napkins, handshakes, and honor.

"Great. You've made the investment; now let's get started." He put the truck into gear and we began to drive through the city. "I'm glad you decided to take the leap of faith and join me in the jungle!" He smiled as if he were a tour guide taking me on an African safari.

"I'll be your jungle guide and it's my job to get you through the jungle of business alive and make sure you avoid all of the deadly predators, traps, diseases, elements, and other things that can kill you. The great part about entering the jungle is that you will be rich if you make it to the other side—I guarantee it. If you can enter, survive, and live long enough to exit the Jungle one day, then you will have more money than you could ever imagine. But you have to do what I say, and promise to make it out alive..."

His words made sense, but I didn't know what to say.

"Do you promise?" he prompted.

"Promise what?" I asked

"Promise me to make it out alive?" He turned to me, black sunglasses shielding his eyes and making him look like a life-sized insect. I couldn't read him because his eyes were hidden; I took a leap of faith and complied:

"I promise." I looked at him with wide eyes, not sure what I had signed up for.

"There are two types of people in the world," explained my jungle guide. "Those who live in the shelter and those who live in the jungle. Most people hide from the real world and are sheltered by their family, their school, their corporate job, or their government. These people rely on an institution or others for survival. That's why they live in the shelter."

"And what about the people who live in the jungle?" I asked.

"People who live in the jungle are exposed to the real world of business; it's a harsh environment and only very skilled entrepreneurs can survive. Not everyone is meant to survive in the jungle though. For most, life is better in the shelter. Only a select few with the desire, the education, the persistence, and the emotional strength are meant to be full-time entrepreneurs and investors. The jungle is filled with predators who will take advantage of you, but the predators aren't the most dangerous part of the jungle."

"What's the most dangerous part of the jungle then?" I asked, as though he wanted me to prompt him to continue.

"You are your own worst enemy when you enter the jungle. Every day I see smart, brave men and women enter the jungle and fail because they haven't mastered the skills required to survive. The predators in the jungle are what everyone is scared of, but realistically, it's we and our lack of survival skills that kill most of us in business."

"What do you mean?" I asked.

"Correct me if I'm wrong, but you recently quit your job, right?"

"Yes," I answered, not sure where he was going.

"How many times have you quit in your life?"

"Three," I answered.

"The first two times you quit your job and entered the jungle; what forced you to go back?" His question pierced into my soul.

"Well, the first two times I didn't know how to sell or run a business… so I guess I couldn't survive in the jungle."

"And tell me about your situation now; why are you here? You have quit your job again and you want my help?"

"Yeah, I'm lost. I know how to sell, raise money, and do deals, but I have no idea how to run a real-estate business, and that's why I'm here." I looked out the window, trying to avoid him.

"Good," said my jungle guide. "You're in the right place. If you do as I say, I'll get you through the jungle alive. Do we have a deal?"

"Yes," I replied. "We have a deal."

SELF MADE LESSONS

1. To achieve your dreams, you may have to travel to other cities to meet the experts. Key people you need to move ahead on your journey will inevitably live in other cities, countries, or continents.

2. There are two worlds in business, the sanctuary and the jungle. Entrepreneurs live in the jungle, where it takes the most difficult to survive and also has the highest rewards.

Visit <u>SelfMadeConfessions.com</u> for more lessons.

Confession #25

BUY, HOLD, AND PRAY
IS BAD BUSINESS

"Many novice real estate investors soon quit the profession and
invest in a well-diversified portfolio of bonds. That's because, when
you invest in real estate, you often see a side of humanity that
stocks, bonds, mutual funds, and saving money shelter you from."

ROBERT KIYOSAKI

We drove downtown and because I had never been to Chicago, my Jungle guide picked a Chicago deep-dish pizza joint for lunch. We sat down in a booth and it was late in the afternoon, so the restaurant was practically empty.

"So tell me," said my jungle guide. "What was your plan in real estate before you met me?"

He left his sunglasses on inside, which annoyed me, but I didn't say anything. "Well, my plan was simple. First, I wanted to buy a single rental house and then double my rental units with every purchase afterward. Next, I would buy a duplex, then double to a fourplex, then double to an eight-plex, and so on. Every deal I wanted to double my units and eventually I would have a huge cash flow and lots of real estate."

"That's a terrible idea," replied my jungle guide, reading a menu.

"Why?" I felt hurt; my plan had got me this far. "What's wrong with my plan?"

"Well, the problem with that plan is that it will take forever to execute and you will have a very hard time gratifying your investors."

"What do you mean?" I asked, picking up a menu.

"You want to grow your business fast and you want to grow it big... If you put your investors into long-term buy-and-hold deals, you won't be able to reuse their money and you will find it hard to grow fast. You're a young guy and I'm sure you want to enjoy your money while you're still young! Why wait until you are fifty or sixty to enjoy your hard work? Let's face it; you would look way better in a red-hot convertible with the top down and a beautiful blonde by your side in your early thirties than you would in your sixties!"

The picture he painted in my mind made his point very clear. Who wanted to be an fat old bald guy in a convertible with a young trophy wife? I needed to learn how to make money now.

"OK." I smiled, putting the pizza menu down. "So how do I build my business fast and gratify investors? I want to have money right away!" I liked the vision he was painting for me and I wanted to know more.

"Very simply, you flip real estate: buy, fix, and sell, just like you see on the TV shows... That's the business model you want. Investors love investing in it, because it's short term, it brings high yields, and it's one of the fastest ways to raise millions of dollars and build a self-sustaining real-estate business."

"But I want to be wealthy, not just have cash!" I objected. "If I'm flipping, I'm not building any wealth. Wealth is obtained through passive income and cash flow."

"Look, I'll show you how cash-flowing properties fit into your business later. No one ever gets rich on cash flow! The key to wealth in real estate is very simple: number one, earn income and number two, invest earned income into passive income. You need to earn income first before you even think of purchasing revenue properties. I want you to think like a fund manager, someone who raises cash, manages the fund, takes some fees, and earns his investors a return. The richest people in the world, like Warren Buffet, raise capital and run a fund. They invest large pools of other people's money and make huge gains through profits and fees. That's what you want to do... Don't make it about the houses, or the doors or the units. That's all garbage anyways. Think about capital under management and returns."

"OK." I said, slowly understanding the shift in thinking. I had become obsessed with the bricks, stick, and dirt of real estate and had failed to see where the real money was made. Managing money was the game I needed to play. I was ready to learn the strategies that the richest people in the world used to make their fortunes.

"Teach me," I said as the waitress brought a round of drinks to our table.

SELF MADE LESSONS

1. Money is all about speed; find ways to gratify your investors fast and encourage them to reinvest often. This will help you grow exponentially.

2. Flipping properties is one of the fastest ways to generate cash in real estate

3. Building wealth in real estate is a two-step process: 1) Earn income. 2) Invest that income into income cash-producing assets.

4. Managing money like a hedge fund is one of the best ways to make big money in real estate through profit sharing and fees.

Visit SelfMadeConfessions.com for more lessons.

Confession #26

SINGLES WIN THE WORLD SERIES

"Yesterday's home runs don't win today's games."

BABE RUTH

"There are two types of deals in real estate," continued my jungle guide, taking a sip of Coke. "Sexy deals and profitable deals. Everyone wants to do sexy deals like land developments, condo developments, luxury homes, vacation homes, and historical restorations, but most of these projects don't make much money."

"What do you mean?" I protested. "Someone must be making money or no one would do them."

"Let me finish…" My jungle guide looked at me, disappointed. "These deals can make money, and they do, when executed by proven professionals. Professionals who do those types of deals as a business can make money, but even then, it can be difficult for them. Most newbies who jump into sexy deals like that go broke, lose their shirts, or barely break even. I can count on my fingers and toes all of my friends and colleagues who were successful with five, ten, or twenty small deals and then decided to go big and got smashed. Going too big too early can ruin your career. My friends who went too big too fast often went bankrupt and are now teaching real-estate classes for big companies to pay the bills." My jungle guide chuckled at their misfortune.

"What do you mean?" I asked, sipping soda water.

"Investing is like baseball and everyone wants to hit a home run because home runs are sexy. But in reality, a home run is statistically the most difficult feat to accomplish in all of sports because the baseball, travelling at 90 miles an hour, has to contact a pin-sized surface area on the bat... it doesn't happen too often."

"But it does happen!" I protested.

"You're right, it happens every once in a while, but most teams who swing for home runs strike out. The other strategy that I prefer is the Moneyball strategy. Did you see the movie *Moneyball*?"

"No I didn't." I stared into my drink, feeling as if I knew nothing.

"It's about this team in Major League Baseball that had a very small budget and they couldn't afford to pay multimillion dollar contracts for home-run hitters. So instead of buying home runs, they bought cheap players who could hit one base. In baseball, four bases add up to a home run and by selecting many cheap players who could all hit singles, this team went on to win the World Series on a shoestring budget.

"With good management, smart math, and one of the smallest budgets in the league, they outperformed teams with the biggest budgets in the world!" My jungle guide grinned ear to ear as if he had just given me the biggest secret in the world.

I leaned back in my seat and let it sink in. I thought he was crazy when I had gotten in the Escalade with him that morning, but now I saw his brilliance.

"Many small things add up to a big thing. Think of it this way: you could do one seventy-five-unit condo building in three years or you could flip twenty-five houses a year for three years. Either way it's seventy-five units and you will make the same money. The difference is that your risk is lower with the seventy-five houses because you aren't taking a long-shot three-year speculation play. With the seventy-five small houses you are in and out fast! In reality, markets go up and markets go down. You and I have no idea what will happen in the next three years. At least with lots of small deals, you aren't betting the farm on hitting one huge home run."

He took another sip of Coke.

"Now of cours," he continued, "not all of your seventy-five flip houses will be great deals, and that's fine. Most you will win, some you will break even on, and some you will lose on, but that's normal for any business. Still, it's better to be diverse and have a high degree of control over seventy-five small, low-risk deals than it is to do one huge high-risk deal. On the big deal you may become a home run or strike out and eat dirt. Go for profitable, not sexy; it rarely pays to be sexy."

SELF MADE LESSONS

1. There are two types of deals: sexy deals and profitable deals.

2. Sexy deals don't usually make money.

3. Many small deals can add up to a big deal.

4. Many small deals have more control than one large deal.

Visit <u>SelfMadeConfessions.com</u> for more lessons.

Confession #27

5 SKILLS OF THE SELF MADE MILLIONAIRE

"There is no such thing as a 'self-made' man.
We are made up of thousands of others."

GEORGE MATTHEW ADAMS

"Okay, I get it," I said, growing impatient with his talks of doing 75 deals over three years. "What do I need to do today to become successful in real estate? I've jumped into the jungle with both feet; I have very little cash, no job, no credit, and a little experience! How am I going to survive?" My question had turned into a desperate rant.

"Let me answer your question with a question." My jungle guide grinned. "Why do most people fail in the jungle and have to go back to their jobs in the sanctuary?"

"Well…" I thought for a moment. "Because they don't have the business skills to survive?"

"Exactly." My jungle guide smiled as he pulled out a napkin. "There are lots of different animals in the jungle and every morning these animals wake up and chase value until they drop dead at night. Some of the animals, like you, are more evolved because you have more skills than the average guy who is brand-new to business. But then there are animals like myself who are more evolved than you. In some ways, there is a food chain and five secrets to becoming a full-time real-estate entrepreneur." As he said these words, my jungle guide spread the napkin like a treasure map to cover as much of the table as possible.

"The first thing I want you to do today is stop calling yourself a Real-Estate Investor… You aren't an investor; you are a Real-Estate Entrepreneur! It's time to change your thinking!"

"OK."

He grabbed a pen and drew a crude diagram of evolution on the napkin.

"I'm going to use the concept of evolution to show you what so many people, including yourself, have been doing wrong in your Entrepreneurial career."

"What have I been doing wrong?" I asked.

"You haven't followed the natural evolution and progression of skills required to survive in the jungle. If you follow the natural progression, running any business, including real estate, is easy. The problem is that most people like you don't build their businesses right and forget to learn some of the major skills."

"So what have I been doing wrong?" I felt like he was drilling the lesson into my skull.

"There are five stages to becoming a fully developed Entrepreneur," he continued. "The first stage, Stage 1, you are a Marketer. In real estate, that's called a bird dog."

"What's a bird dog?" I asked, not familiar with the term.

"A Bird Dog is a hunting term for a dog that would run through the forest and collect dead ducks and other birds that his master had shot down with his rifle. In real estate, a bird dog is someone who advertises, collects leads, and sells them to other investors for profit. These people are pure marketers and understand lead flow."

"OK…" I took a sip of soda.

"After you have become a competent Bird Dog, you graduate to becoming a Negotiator. In real estate, that's called a Wholesaler. You have heard of Wholesalers before, right?"

"Yeah, those are guys who buy houses under contract with no money and sell the contracts to other investors for profit."

"That's right," said my jungle guide. "Since most Bird Dogs have leads, the next skill they must learn is to negotiate and sell. They need to learn to negotiate with the motivated sellers to get the lowest possible price for a property and then sell their purchase contracts to other investors. If a bird dog doesn't learn to negotiate and sell, then he will stay as a marketer his whole life. The sad thing is that most people don't know how to sell or negotiate, so they never really do well when they jump into real estate."

"Why don't most people know how to sell or negotiate?" I asked, trying to grasp the concept of why so many fail.

"I think it's because we live in a society that frowns upon negotiating and haggling for prices and the things that we really want. We are far too polite and accept prices as written. As far as selling goes, I think that most people never learn to sell because they think that sales is slimy or crooked. The truth is that everyone wants to buy, but no one wants to be sold. Most people have negative beliefs selling their ideas or taking money from other people regardless of how good their product or service is."

"OK, so what's the next stage after marketing and negotiating?" I asked.

"Stage 3 occurs when an entrepreneur has mastered the art of marketing and negotiating to become a producer. In your real-estate business, Stage 3 would be a flipping business. Instead of flipping, I like to call it the buy-fix-sell strategy. Unfortunately, everybody thinks that flipping houses is sexy and easy so this is the stage that most people jump into. The average guy figures he can swing hammers and paint walls, so why not flip a house? Unfortunately, I buy houses from many of these ignorant people who jump into the deep end with two feet and fail because they didn't understand the skills it took to become a profitable producer. A Stage 3 business, a production business, takes a lot of time, money, and risk. Not everybody should jump into production without mastering marketing and negotiating first."

"So what are the new skills for Stage 3?" I asked.

"Very simple. In Stage 1, you learned to market and generate leads. In Stage 2, you learned to sell and negotiate. In Stage 3, you need to learn production and finance. Production in the context of flipping houses is managing construction crews and knowing which renovations are profitable and which ones lose money. Finance is the skill of getting these purchase contracts funded. A Stage-2 wholesaler can negotiate and sell profitable real-estate contracts all day long, but he won't get to Stage 3 until he learns how to finance these contracts and get them funded. Of course, most people fail at Stage 3 because they decide to save money by fixing houses themselves. If you fix the house yourself, you will never learn to manage the production of others and you will stay small forever. Most people also get held back by trying to finance every deal themselves with their own money, which keeps them from learning about all of the other great financing options out there."

"So what's next?" I asked.

"Stage 4 is another stage that most people jump straight into and fail hard at. I call it buy-and-hold, but other people call it rental properties or income properties. This stage is for people who have made money in Stage 1, Stage 2, and Stage 3 businesses and now need to protect and grow their profits. Most people fail at this stage because they don't bother to learn Stage 1, Stage 2, and Stage 3 and then they jump in to Stage 4 with no skills. If you are stuck in your business, it means that you lack some critical skills!

"The main skill for Stage 4 is being able to control cash-flowing assets. If a real-estate entrepreneur can spot trends in the market and figure out which neighborhoods are going to have the highest amount of appreciation while creating cash flow, he can get filthy stinking rich in Stage 4. But unfortunately, most people don't get rich in Stage 4 because they don't bother to learn the skills."

"I think I see what I did wrong." I stared into the bubbles of my drink. "I think I jumped in at Stage 4 and tried to buy-hold-and-pray my way to success."

"From what you told me earlier about the deals you've done, it sounds like you did."

"I didn't bother to learn the skills of marketing, negotiation, sales, production, finance, or even how to buy cash-flowing assets properly. I just jumped right in and now I'm stuck and feeling the pain." I felt stupid and wanted to bang my head on the table.

"Don't worry about it," said the jungle guide. "You are way ahead of most people who try to strike out and become an entrepreneur. You have tried, made some mistakes, made some money, and you are here to get straightened out. Don't worry; by the end of our time together, I'll have you pointed in the right direction!"

"OK," I said, looking up at him slowly. "What's the last stage?"

"Stage 5 is what I like to call the Capitalist stage. This is for seasoned investors who control millions of dollars of cash. They can fund lots of deals, either buy-fix-sell or buy-and-hold, and these people, because they have so much cash, are the king of the jungle. There are two ways to become a capitalist. Number one is to make money through Stage 1 through 4 and save up over the years, but that's the slow way. The fast way is to go out and raise capital, build a fund with other people's money, and dominate the market! That's what I want you to do…"

"Aren't capitalists evil?" I whined.

"Capitalists are people who raise capital and do business with it. I'm not here to make political judgments about words or semantics; I'm just here to make money. Let go of your limiting beliefs about capitalism and money; you'll thank me when you do. Plus, no one makes money without providing value or doing good. I'm going to make sure that you provide so much value to the world that it will be impossible to ever be broke again!"

SELF MADE LESSONS

1. Most people fail to survive in the jungle because they don't have the skills of the entrepreneur. These skills are secrets to the poor and the middle class, namely 1) Marketing, 2) Negotiating, 3) Production, 4) Cash-Flowing Assets, and 5) Capital Raising.

2. If you learn these entrepreneurial skills in the right order, then building your business will be much easier than someone who tries to build it out of order.

Visit <u>SelfMadeConfessions.com</u> for more lessons.

Confession #28

SECRET #1: YOU MUST BECOME A FANTASTIC MARKETER

"Marketing is a contest for people's attention."

SETH GODIN

"Let's eat!" said my jungle guide, plunging into a huge slice of pepperoni and sausage deep-dish pizza. The pizza was piping hot and a veil of steam covered his face. He picked up his pizza and ate with his hands while I picked at my piece with a fork.

"So tell me more about these skills that I'm missing…" I was less interested with the pizza and more interested in fixing my problems.

"Alright. So let's go back to the beginning. The first skill you have to learn is that of a marketer. What's the lifeblood of any business?" He quizzed me with a mouth full of pizza.

"I don't know… Money?" I guessed, looking up at him.

"Wrong; that's why you have problems. The lifeblood of any business is leads! So many businesses struggle or go bankrupt because they don't have enough leads walking in the door or the phone doesn't ring enough. If you have leads, you have customers and money; if you don't have leads, then you will eventually go broke."

"So how do I get leads and get my lifeblood pumping?" I put my fork down.

"There are two major ways to get leads in any business, including real estate. Getting leads is the same whether you are buying and selling high-end mansions in Beverly Hills or ghetto houses in Winnipeg. All business-es get new leads through 1) Local Marketing and 2) Internet Marketing. Local marketing will get you a better quality lead and you are more likely to get a customer, but Internet marketing will get you a better flow and potentially cheaper leads through online classified ads on kijiji.com or craigslist.com."

"So what kind of signs do I put up?"

"You have probably seen those ugly, yellow, plastic signs that read WE BUY HOUSES with a phone number 555-5555. Those are other bird dogs and real-estate investors who are looking for distressed sellers. The crazy part is that those signs work. Those signs work every day of the week and some of my best deals come from those signs."

"Who would anyone ever want to call one of those signs?" I asked, leaning back in my seat and feeling skeptical.

"Well, that's a good question," said my jungle guide, forking another slice of pizza. "You would think that most people would call Realtors to sell their homes, but the sellers who call the WE BUY HOUSES signs are peo-ple who are in trouble. It's much like the same crowd that responds to WE BUY GOLD advertisements or the pawnshop crowd. These people maybe talked to a Realtor and their house is too dirty or too damaged and the Realtor didn't want it. Or maybe the Realtor wanted repairs done before he listed the house. For whatever reason, these people want to talk to you, and you need to reach them with local signs and Internet advertising."

"So what do I do when someone calls?" I asked.

"Well, you are a little more advanced than the average investor I talk to, so you'll probably go see the lead yourself and likely sign up a deal to fix and flip the house or some other strategy. But what I advise most novice investors to do is to sell the lead to another investor for twenty to five hundred dollars."

"Sell the lead?" I couldn't believe what I was hearing. "You mean people buy leads?"

"All the time! That's what marketing businesses do!" exclaimed my jungle guide. "I have bird dogs that I pay twenty dollars to every time they bring me a name and phone number and if I close on the deal, I'll pay them five hundred. It's worth it to me; I'll make ten, twenty, thirty, or even fifty grand on the deal. Why not pay the guy five hundred bucks? It takes money to make money. I even know some really organized marketers who have built lead service companies and they will sell leads to entrepreneurs and Realtors alike for a small monthly subscription fee of thirty dollars a month or they will sell them piece-by-piece for twenty to a hundred dollars each. If these marketers sign up three hundred Realtors to the subscription service and send out leads or lead lists as they come in, thirty dollars times three hundred is nine thousand dollars a month in passive income. What does it cost to run a marketing service like that?"

"I'm not sure," I replied. "Not much, just labor and a computer."

"Bingo." My jungle guide smiled. "Sometimes there is more money in the services related to real estate than there is in real estate itself. If you want to be rich, you have to think outside the box."

SELF MADE CONFESSIONS

1. Leads are the lifeblood of any business, not just money.

2. Leads come from two general sources: local marketing and Internet marketing.

3. Local marketing is surprisingly effective. Bandit signs that read WE BUY HOUSES are inconvenient to use, but yield very high-quality leads.

4. Bird dogs (mini marketing companies) can sell private leads for $20–$500 per lead.

5. Bird dogs can also open a lead subscription service and sell leads for a monthly fee. Another structure to sell leads is a private lead agreement of 50 or 100 leads to a single Realtor or investor.

6. There is sometimes more money in the services related to real estate than there is in the deals themselves!

Visit SelfMadeConfessions.com for more lessons.

Confession #29

SECRET #2: YOU MUST BECOME A MASTER NEGOTIATOR

"Income rarely exceeds personal development."

JIM ROHN

"So I become king of the bird-dogs… Then what?" I asked with a smirk as I cut into my slice of pizza.

"Don't knock bird dogs; these people are very important! You have to master marketing if you want to become a successful entrepreneur! But to answer your question, the next skill you need to learn is to become a master negotiator and learn to sell!"

"Negotiation is by far the most valuable skill in any business, including real estate, because every single business interaction is a negotiation. In real estate, there is no inherent profit in any property. People who have mastered the art of negotiation can build profit into any deal. I was reviewing my numbers from last year and it shocked me to see that every single dollar of profit I earned in my real-estate business was profit that I negotiated into the deal. Had I not negotiated, I wouldn't have made a cent in the entire year!"

"Wow," I said under my breath. "So if most people don't know how to negotiate, then they won't make any money in real estate?"

"Yes! That's true. Most people fail at negotiation and some of my students will call me whining that they can't find a deal. In truth, there are only three ways to find a deal: 1) Networking, 2) Marketing, and 3) Negotiating. I spend lots of time and money every year studying to become a better negotiator. Every time I increase my negotiation kills, I also earn more money in my businesses!"

"So if I wanted to become a full-time negotiator or a property wholesaler, what kind of money could I expect to make?" I asked, poking at my pizza that was now getting cold.

"Well, wholesalers make roughly ten times what a bird dog would make. Instead of making five hundred a deal, I'll pay my wholesalers roughly five grand a deal and it's worth every penny."

"Five thousand dollars?" I objected, spitting out a bite of pizza. "That's a lot of money!"

"And it's a lot of work! The wholesaler not only has to do the marketing job of a bird dog, but he also has to go meet the distressed seller and negotiate the price low enough to be profitable. It's a hard job and it's worth $5,000 a deal if you are going to make $15,000, $25,000, or $35,000 on the deal. You have to stop being so cheap and start thinking of ways to pay people. When you pay people, they will do the work for you so you can focus on building a better machine and becoming a better entrepreneur."

"Pay more to make more? That doesn't make sense to me; if I spend more, won't I have less?"

"No, no, no… You have to get rid of your scarcity mentality. If you paid $5,000 for a deal that made you $15,000, how many deals could you afford to do?"

"As many as I could get my hands on," I said with a smile.

"Exactly!" retorted my jungle guide. "You want to be smart about how you spend your money as a real-estate entrepreneur. Money is infinite and it flows through the hands of the people who have mastered it. You need to become one of those people who can spend five thousand on a wholesale contract and make fifteen thousand every day of the week. There's nothing wrong with tripling your money and doing very little work. Wholesalers are very valuable. Treat them well, pay them well, and you will be swimming in cash before you know it."

SELF MADE CONFESSIONS

1. Most real-estate deals have no inherent profit in them. Most profits in real estate come from negotiating your profit onto the table.

2. Deals come from three activites: 1) Networking, 2) Marketing, and 3) Negotiating.

3. Negotiation is a skill that no one is born with. We all have to learn to negotiate, like riding a bike. Take classes, read books, and practice in live situations to boost your negotiation skills.

4. Paying a wholesaler $5,000 per deal is worth it if you are going to make $15,000.

5. It takes money to make money; paying for an opportunity is sometimes the best way to go.

Visit <u>SelfMadeConfessions.com</u> for more lessons.

Confession #30

SECRET #3: YOU MUST MAKE AMAZING PRODUCTS

"It's tangible, it's solid, it's beautiful. It's artistic, from my standpoint, and I just love real estate."

DONALD TRUMP

"There are three types of money in real estate," said my jungle guide. "Fast Money, Big Money, and Passive Money. We already talked about wholesaling, which is the fast money; now let's talk about the Big Money… Buy-Fix-Sell."

My eyes grew wide, loving the idea of the big money and wanting to know more.

"So wholesalers and bird dogs are making money off real estate with literally zero cash, zero credit, and in some ways, zero experience. They have no risk and they don't even really need to know if the deal is good or not, and why should they care? They don't have any skin in the game. At Stage 3 though, when you become a buy-fix-sell guy, now you have to know how to analyze the deal, fund the deal, and renovate it profitably. As a skill set, your skills just became exponentially more valuable and that's why you're going to make the big money instead of the fast money. Big skills equal big money; fast skills equal fast money."

"The good news is," continued my jungle guide, "if you build your skills properly, you will have lead flow coming in the door from your marketing skills and you will also have profitable deals coming in the door from your negotiating skills. All you have to do at this point is to stop selling these contracts to other investors and start doing the deals yourself."

"Do the deals myself? Like hammering my own nails and painting my own walls?" I asked.

"No, you don't want to do the $10 per hour jobs yourself, but you do want to fund the deal, manage a general contractor, and make sure the property is sold quickly to make a profit. Stage 3, creating amazing products, is where real estate becomes a full-blown business and you become a true entrepreneur. You are also going to be making big money! Where marketers are earning five hundred dollars a deal, negotiators are earning $5,000 a deal; you will be earning fifteen grand a deal by becoming a retailer and bringing amazing products to market. It's a big jump in income, and also a big jump in skills. You will be managing time, large amounts of money, team members, employees, stress, and risk. Flipping houses is big money and big risk, but I assure you that it's one of my favorite ways to make money in real estate."

"I understand that I get paid more for having more skills... but why is there more money in flipping houses than wholesaling or bird dogging?" I asked, thinking about the numbers.

"Great question.," replied my jungle guide. "There is more money in flipping houses because we are starting to unlock the true power of real estate. All rich people use leverage to achieve more results with less effort. Leverage allows us to earn more money. Where an average man will try to move a thousand-pound boulder with his bare hands, a man who understands leverage will use a fulcrum and a long lever to move boulders larger than he could ever imagine. Archimedes, the Greek mathematician, once said, "Give me a lever long enough, and a fulcrum on which to place it, and I shall move the world."

"So I need to use leverage to get rich?" I asked.

"Yes, absolutely! The only way to get rich in anything is to use some kind of leverage! Flippers begin to unlock the power of real estate because they begin to use the leverage of finance and 'other people's money' to earn bigger profits than bird dogs or wholesalers. Generally in investing, the higher the leverage, the more money you can borrow, the higher the profits can be. Consequently, the higher the leverage, the more money you can lose as well. This is why some say: 'The greater the risk, the greater the reward.'"

"You mean in buy-fix-sell I could actually lose money?" I gulped, thinking of my potential losses.

"Of course," replied my jungle guide. "With the ability to make great profits comes a great responsibility. When a flipper investor borrows another person's money, he has an obligation to return that money safely. The ability to finance deals with other people's money is a privilege that very few investors enjoy. To ensure that the borrowed money comes back safely, these highly skilled investors must be able to analyze deals for safety, speed, and profitability."

"You mean not all real-estate deals are the same?" I asked, taking a sip of soda.

"There are deals that can be profitable but are not safe to invest in. There are deals that are safe to invest in but aren't profitable. Don't get those two types of deals mixed up. Typically, my investment philosophy follows that of Warren Buffet, the world's richest investor. Buffet's first rule of investing is, 'Don't lose money.' Buffet's second rule of investing is, 'Always obey rule #1.'"

SELF MADE LESSONS

1. Flipping properties is natural if you have built your skills as a marketer and a negotiator.

2. Stop selling leads and contracts and start funding them yourself!

3. Flipping properties is the big money strategy in real estate. Expect to earn five-figure profits.

4. Flipping properties uses leverage, which is other people's money. Leverage is a technique of controlling more resources with less.

5. Unlike Stage 1 and Stage 2, in Stage 3, you can actually lose money on your deals! Be careful to select the right opportunities! Don't be reckless with other people's money.

Visit <u>SelfMadeConfessions.com</u> for more lessons.

Confession #31

SECRET #4: YOU MUST CONTROL CASH-FLOWING ASSETS

"Don't follow trends, start trends."

FRANK CAPRA

"So I make fast money wholesaling houses and big money flipping houses; what's next?" I asked my jungle guide.

"Now you must control cash-flowing assets! If you make it this far in your real-estate business, then you have now proved yourself as a money-making machine and you are earning a sizable amount of cash. It's time to invest that cash into cash-flowing assets and create long-term wealth! The fourth stage of any business is to control cash-flowing assets, but unfortunately this type of business is screwed up badly by most people."

"Why do most people screw up cash-flowing assets?"

"Well, it's very simple. Making money in cash-flowing assets is all about trend spotting. A smart entrepreneur that can see trends as they happen or before they happen can make a lot of money in transitional zones and neighborhoods that others wouldn't see potential in."

"You mean like slums or derelict parts of town? I don't want to invest in those areas; I don't want to be a slumlord!" I objected.

"Well, not exactly. I'm not talking about the war zone; I'm talking about areas that might be a little scary today, but in five years, maybe these neighborhoods will be cool, hip, or exciting to live in: areas that are gentrifying and areas where the government or private–public partnerships are investing big dollars. You see, you should be able to make a hundred grand per deal over time if you buy right and manage your properties as a cash-flow investor. If you buy the right property in the right neighborhood with the right management and the right finance, this is one of the best ways to get filthy stinking rich!"

"OK, so how do most people screw up cash-flow investing?"

"Well, many people buy their rental properties in areas that are already mature, areas that don't have any room to improve or areas that they would want to live in. While those deals are sexy deals, they don't necessarily make the massive equity gains that we all want in real estate. In fact, those types of houses in mature neighborhoods could very likely lose money over time."

"So you mean I can't just invest for cash flow, buy any house in any neighborhood, and make money?"

"No, you can't unfortunately," replied my jungle guide. "No one has ever got rich off cash flow. Instead, you get rich on equity, so you need to find areas that will appreciate over time and collect cash flow while you hold the assets. Don't get me wrong; cash flow is great and a cash-flowing business can build a strong monthly income of ten or twenty grand a month. Big healthy cash flows are nice, and if you can build a big cash flow, you will begin to see the benefits of having long-term wealth. Some of these benefits are: more family time, more time off, less stress, less poking around in houses, and dealing with contractors. You just have to make sure you spot the trends right so in five or ten years after buying your properties, you are making a hundred thousand dollars in equity gains per house instead a meager ten thousand per house. Passive money is good, but why not grab some big money as well?"

SELF MADE CONFESSIONS

1. Passive money in business comes from owning cash-flowing assets. In real estate, this strategy is called buy-and-hold.

2. Invest in transitional zones, areas that are scary today but will be desirable in five years. These areas yield the greatest appreciation.

3. Avoid the "war zone" or the slums; those areas rarely change because the demographics are unchanging. The bottom is the bottom.

4. Follow big government investment as well as private–public partnerships. You might as well make the government your partner.

5. Three things are needed for success with this strategy: 1) right neighborhood, 2) right management, and 3) right financing.

6. With this strategy you can make up to $100,000 a deal over time; this is one of the ways to get filthy stinking rich.

7. You can build a strong cash flow of $10,000 to $20,000 over time and start to reap the benefits of passive investing.

Visit <u>SelfMadeConfessions.com</u> for more lessons.

Confession #32

SECRET #5: YOU MUST RAISE CAPITAL AND BECOME A CAPITALIST

"Rule No. 1: Never lose money.
Rule No. 2: Never forget rule No.1."

WARREN BUFFETT

"I've saved the best for last," said my jungle guide as if he had a secret to tell me. "It's one thing to survive in the jungle; it's another thing to thrive. I like your hustle, I like your questions, and I want you to thrive."

"Thanks," I said.

"You can always see the intelligence in a person based on the questions they ask; you ask good questions and you get good answers. But let me tell you about my secret weapon."

I leaned in, waiting to hear his secret.

"I want you to become king of the jungle, so you need to become a capitalist. Stage-5 real-estate investors are the undisputed kings and queens of the jungle. Where there might be hundreds of bird dogs swarming around and dozens of wholesalers, usually there are only a handful of Stage-5 real-estate entrepreneurs in the jungle."

"Why are there so few?"

"Well, good question. There are very few Stage-5 investors because these investors have large amounts of liquid capital; millions of dollars ready to do deals at any given time. That's why they are the kings and queens of the jungle. They can fund any deal at any time and they can do it all cash."

"Whoa," I whispered in disbelief.

"That's right. These investors have so much money that they can do dozens, even hundreds of deals every year and they dominate their markets. Some of these investors run out of deals to fund and will get into hard money lending as another source of income, but I'm not here to talk about lending with you."

"Well, I don't have millions of dollars, so I can't become a capitalist," I objected.

"Well, that's not necessarily true. What do Warren Buffet, world's richest investor, and Donald Trump, the real-estate billionaire, have in common?"

"That's easy." I laughed. "They're rich!"

"That's true, they are rich, but they became rich by raising money. They don't use their own money for their deals, they are capitalists operating at Stage 5 and that's how they became billionaires!"

I let his words sink in. "So I guess I have to become a capitalist if I want to be rich in real estate."

My jungle guide grinned from ear to ear. "It's time to become a capitalist."

REAL-LIFE LESSONS FROM THIS CONFESSION

1. The king of the jungle is the capitalist investor with millions of dollars of liquid capital to invest.

2. Warren Buffet and Donald Trump, two of the world's richest investors, raise money to do their deals; why don't you?

Visit <u>SelfMadeConfessions.com</u> for more lessons.

Confession #33

WHY YOU MUST BECOME A CAPITALIST

"More valuable than a thousand days of study is
one day with a great teacher."

JAPANESE PROVERB

"So... It's almost time for me to leave," said my jungle guide. It was getting dark outside. "How many deals do you want to do?

"One hundred." I choked. "... I want to do a hundred deals this year." The number "100" was a completely arbitrary number; I had just picked it out of the air because it sounded great and I was feeling ready to take on the world.

"A hundred deals? That's a lot of deals. Are you sure you want to do that?"

I wasn't sure at all, but I lied. "Yes!" I said, sounding more confident.

"Alright, how much cash are you going to need to buy, fix, and sell a single house in your area?"

This number I was sure of. "A hundred to two hundred thousand dollars," I replied.

There was a short pause at his end and I could tell that he was doing some quick mental math. "You're going to need three to five milllion in cash to do that. And you need to raise it all from no more than two people."

Three million to five million in cash? I couldn't believe what he just said.

Every real-estate transaction I had done to date was done with small amounts of cash and large mortgages from traditional banks. The idea of finding five million dollars of cash from one or two people seemed incredible and impossible.

"You can do it," he assured me. "You've done some deals before; it's simple. You are just going to do them a little differently… all cash, no banks, and you are just going to be doing more deals than you are now. Trust me, it's leverage. We are going to take a small, simple strategy—flipping houses and repeat it one hundred times. There isn't a lot of risk in a simple business model like that and there are lots of millionaires out there who want to invest with young hungry guys like you."

I couldn't believe his words. Everything he said challenged my belief systems and I wanted to resist him. I wanted to tell him that everything he was telling me could not be done. The lazy man inside me wanted to run from the table and lie on my mother's couch while I slipped into comfortable denial. The ambitious man inside me wanted to believe everything he said was true. Looking back, the only reason why I believed anything he said was I literally had no other option.

My head had been forced under water for far too long and money, my oxygen, was running out. Instead of listening to my fears, which were telling me to resist and reject him, I had to take his word on faith—faith that what he was saying was real.

Up to this point in my real-estate investing career, I had raised small amounts of cash from friends and family and I remembered the moment when I stopped failing and started succeeding. I had tried to raise money by shyly asking people I knew for money with a single business plan, but nothing more. Since I was disorganized in my own thoughts and presentation, I had scared every potential investor away. When I changed my approach and began to ask for money with a typed business proposition in a proper format, I started to see success with small investors and everything changed.

"I guess I better make a business plan?" I asked, thinking back to my prior success in raising money for real estate.

"Well, no," he replied. "The people you are looking for are rich. They don't care about your business plan. They will do their own numbers and analysis to make sure you are legit. Sure, you can write one up for your own understanding of the business, but sophisticated investors don't care about your businesses plan and will never read it.

Think about it; if you're a rich guy, do you want to spend the evening reading some kid's crappy business plan? Or do you want to spend the evening with your wife and daughter? These people are rich; they invest with you because they don't have the time to do the deals themselves. Their time is extremely valuable and they don't want their time wasted!"

"So what do I show them?" I asked. I felt a deep need to bring something tangible to the table for a big-fish investor.

"Well, it's simple. People invest with you for two reasons: 1) They believe in you and 2) they believe in your business model. It's as simple as that. Screw your business plan, screw pages of financial projections, screw the stuff they teach you at business school!"

I began to feel uncomfortable as he tore apart every single belief I had about raising money. But I had dropped out of business school, so I felt like I fit in with his advice.

"There are two parts to this," he continued. "First, you have to make them like you and believe in you. You must position yourself as the expert. Second, you have to be able to explain your entire business on a cocktail napkin."

"A napkin?" I exclaimed. "You're kidding! I can't raise millions of dollars on a cocktail napkin! That will never work!"

"It works all the time; trust me; I do it all the time. If you can't explain your business model on a napkin in a way that a three-year-old child will understand, then you don't understand your business and don't deserve to raise any money."

"OK," I said reluctantly, "how do I explain my business model on a napkin and make it make sense to a three-year-old?"

"Easy," he replied. "Take a piece of paper and fold it over twice so it's small like a cocktail napkin."

I tore a sheet of paper out of my binder and folded it twice so it was one quarter of its original size, barely larger than a cocktail napkin. "OK, now what?"

"A billionaire taught me this, so listen carefully. You need to explain your business in pennies; you need to make a penny budget. A three-year-old understands pennies and so do rich people. Write this down:

> Buy all properties at 40 to 60 cents on the dollar
> Renovate up to 70 cents
> Sell at 100 cents
> It will cost you 10 cents to sell
> You net 20 cents
> You split the 20 cents with your investor
> You each get 10 cents

I scribbled his words onto my napkin and it seemed too simple. "How do I apply this to actual real estate?"

"Very simple; the pennies are percentages and whether you are fixing and selling a crack house for fifty grand, or a mansion worth a million dollars, the ratios and percentages are always the same. Your investors will love you for making such a complicated business simple to understand, and as long as you stay within those ratios, you will be profitable. You want to sell your investors the business model—not the individual deal! If you sell them the deal, they are going to be overwhelmed by details and find a reason to not do business with you. Let's do an example:

> Buy a house at 50 cents on the dollar = $100,000
> Renovate up to 70 cents = $140,000 ($100,000 buy plus $40,000 renovation)
> Sell at 100 cents = $200,000 After Repair Value
> It will cost you 10 cents to sell = $20,000 (fees, Realtors, etc.)
> You net 20 cents = $40,000
> You split the 20 cents with your investor = $40,000 profit to split
> You each get 10 cents = $20,000 net profit each

If you sell them on the business model and prove that every deal you bring fits the model, then they will never say no. Think about it; you know more about real estate than they do, and that's why you are going to be the one picking the deals and making the big dollars. If they knew real estate better than you and had the advantage of available time, then they wouldn't need you. Right?"

"You're right." I agreed.

"You can stay small and do a few deals per year. Or you can keep your job and own a few small rental houses. Or you can even own a few small apartment buildings, but there's only one fast way to make it out of the rat race and onto the fast track... and that is to become a capitalist."

"A capitalist? Aren't those the people that ruin the environment and make their employees work for less money? Aren't capitalists responsible for everything wrong in the world?" I asked.

"It depends on how you define capitalist. I define a capitalist as someone who raises capital and does business with it. If you want to survive in the real world as an entrepreneur, you must learn to become a capitalist because raising capital is the number one skill of the entrepreneur. Too many real entrepreneurs fail or can't get out of their jobs because they don't know how to raise enough capital to support their business and their family. Every investor runs out of money at some point and even billionaires like Warren Buffet or Donald Trump raise capital for their ventures. If you are going to get rich, you have to get rich by using someone else's money." With those words, he got up to leave, but before he did, he wrote down one final piece of wisdom on a napkin and handed it to me.

It read:

Your Winning Business Model
Raise $5,000,000; earn a 20% return on investment every year.
Earn this return hitting singles (flipping small houses)
20% Return is $1,000,000 in profit; split it with your investors.
Your investors make a 10% return on their money and
You take the other 10% or $500,000 in profit every year.
After two years, you will be a cash millionaire.

He pushed the napkin to me and left the restaurant.

SELF MADE CONFESSIONS:

1. You need $3,000,000 to $5,000,000 in cash to dominate your local market. Perhaps more or less depending on the size of your market.

2. A simple strategy repeated 100 times will yield huge results. Think of McDonalds; they have executed the simple strategy of selling $1 cheeseburgers one billion times!

3. There are many millionaire investors who are actively looking to provide funding for hungry ambitious entrepreneurs. The investors provide all the cash, the entrepreneurs provide all of the work, and the profits are shared.

4. Many wealthy and successful people don't want to read a big and bulky business plan. They want something quick and easy to get the point across. Make your presentation direct and to the point. If they like your plan, they will do their own due diligence.

5. Investors invest in two things: 1) you as a person and 2) your system for making money.

6. You must be able to explain your system on a cocktail napkin, or they will lose interest.

7. Sell your investors the business model, not the individual deals, or they will be confused.

8. Raising capital is the #1 skill of the entrepreneur.

Visit <u>SelfMadeConfessions.com</u> for more lessons.

FINAL THOUGHTS

What does it take to become a Self Made Millionaire? Many have wondered, but few have persisted. To become Self Made, we need a definite vision and the perseverance to make our dreams a reality. A man can go from zero to Self Made millionaire in five years if he is focused, determined, and has the right mentor. We live in a wonderful time where it is easier and faster than ever to become rich. If an ordinary man is able to master and apply the skills of marketing, negotiating, production, cash-flowing assets, and raising capital, then he will have opened the floodgates to great riches. He may lose his fortune in the pursuit of wealth, but he will never lose his skills.

All wealth is of the heart and mind and not of the pocket.

Self-made millionaires who have mastered specialized knowledge can make or lose their fortune many times over. The spirit that made a fortune once can make it over and over again. Money never can make you rich; instead applied knowledge makes you rich. Modern-day alchemists, those who turn lead into gold, pull money out of thin air through the execution and sale of their ideas. These modern-day magicians understand that money is just an idea. To have money, we must become rich first in our minds by accumulating specialized knowledge. Second, we must become rich through the application and monetization of specialized knowledge. Only a select few choose to understand that money is only an idea and become the masters of money. In contrast, the vast majority believes that money is a physical commodity, their absolute master and must be earned through sacrifice of blood, sweat, and tears.

Free your mind, and then free your wallet. I wish you all the best on your Self Made journey. If there is any way I can be of service to you, please contact my office through StefanAarnio.com

Respect The Grind,

Stefan Aarnio

Give a man a fish and he's fed for a day.
Teach a man to fish and he's fed for life.
Teach a man to teach fishermen and end world hunger!

EXCLUSIVE BONUSES

1. BONUS VIDEO: How To Attract Big Investors and Big Money – Learn the Secrets Used To Get Millions Of Dollars Behind Your Ideas! ($97 Value)

2. BONUS VIDEO: Multiple Streams Of Income – Learn How The Rich Get Richer By Using Multiple Streams Of Income ($97 Value)

3. BONUS VIDEO: How to Make Massive Profits In Real Estate – Learn How To Time The Market And Invest With The Lowest Risk And Highest Returns ($97 Value)

4. BONUS TEST: Find Your Personal Best Strategy For Making Money In Real Estate – Find The Easiest And Fastest Way To Profit Regardless Of Your Personal Situation! ($47 Value)

Go to <u>SelfMadeConfessions.com</u> to claim your bonuses!

THE IMPORTANCE OF HAVING A COACH

Dear Reader:

If you are serious about taking your real-estate or business career to the next level, then it is absolutely imperative that you have a coach. In my life I struggled when I tried to reinvent the wheel and improvise in business by myself. You are in business for yourself, but you shouldn't be in business by yourself! An investment in a coach can make all of the difference between wild success and crushing defeat. If you are ready to take your business to the next level, consider hiring a coach. At the time of writing, I have four coaches guiding me toward greater success.

Respect The Grind,

Stefan Aarnio

To enquire about coaching, please visit stefanaarnio.com/coaching for a complimentary strategy session!

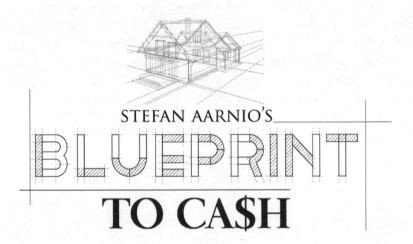

STEFAN AARNIO'S

BLUEPRINT
TO CA$H

To get Stefan Aarnio's blueprint to cash
visit **blueprinttocash.com**

PRAISE FOR SELF MADE:

"Stefan Aarnio is living proof that the American dream is still alive! Anyone can start out with nothing and become SELF MADE!"
>WAYNE ALLYN ROOT
>*Former US Vice-Presidential Nominee*
>*National Best-Selling Author*

"Frankly Stefan Aarnio pisses me off... Why? He's so damn smart (and wise) for such a young guy! Joking aside, if you are looking for an example of how to start with nothing and reach your dreams FAST, *Self Made* will help you do exactly that...become 'Self Made'. Read it. Get inspired by it. Then go out and DO it!"
>DAVE DUBEAU
>*Real Estate Investor, Trainer, Author*

"Stefan's book will help all entrepreneurs to ignite their dreams."
>TAMMY KLING
>*Best-Selling Author, Futurist*

"Stefan Aarnio is a great story teller and has a fantastic story to tell. Many can learn from his mistakes and successes in *Self Made*."
>TONY JEARY
>*The RESULTS Guy*

"*Self Made* is easy to read and a guide for anyone wishing to go from zero to millionaire."
>DOUGLAS VERMEEREN
>*Author of* Guerilla Achiever

"*Self Made* is not just a book about making it in real estate, it's about making it in life!"
>ROSS ALEX
>*FlippingInAction.com*

"Stop and listen. Stefan Aarnio expresses ideas in a way that will make you understand. His story is inspiring and he delivers value, plain and simple."
>JASON GRESCHUK
>*President of Stratford Price*

"If you want a starting point with easy to follow examples and a step-by-step guide for how to make money in Real Estate, then this is a fantastic read... Stefan's 'Self Made Lessons' at the end of each chapter should be written onto yellow sticky notes and taped all over your home and office. Informative and engaging read!"

AARON ADAMS
Alpine Capital Solutions

"*Self Made* is a well-deserved title for Stefan's new book. Unlike many business authors of today, Stefan is a true operator who actively practices what he preaches and has learned the unique, challenging, and valuable lessons that it takes to truly become a self made entrepreneur."

DEAN SUTTON
President Sutton Industries

"Wow! I enjoyed Stefan's first book; this one is even better! In *Self Made*, Stefan made me relive his entrepreneurial journey—mine was very similar—all with emotional hurdles, mentors' guidance, and timeless business lessons. If you are thinking of starting a business, this book is like a telescope that gives you a glance into your future. It shows you how to prepare for the events to come and how to overcome entrepreneurial obstacles. As I always say: 'Business is Simple; Entrepreneurs are Delusional!' Stefan really conquered the delusion, his journey and his successes are proofs of it. This book is a must-read for all would-be entrepreneurs!

MARCO ROBERT
Author of The Business Intervention

"Most money books are a snore-fest; this one held my attention right until the end!"

SHELLY HAGEN
Di-Rae Developments

"*Self Made* delivers financial wisdom wrapped in an entertaining story!"

QUENTIN D'SOUZA
Author of The Ultimate Wealth Strategy

MORE BOOKS BY
THE AUTHOR

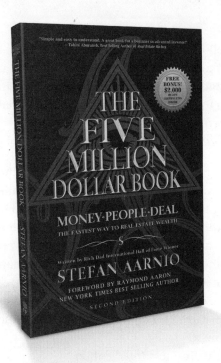

To Order, go to <u>TheFiveMillionDollarBook.com</u>

For a full list of products and to book
speaking engagements, please visit
<u>stefanaarnio.com</u>